P9-CER-517

TWAYNE'S WORLD AUTHORS SERIES

A Survey of the World's Literature

Sylvia E. Bowman, Indiana University

GENERAL EDITOR

CHINA

Howard S. Levy

EDITOR

Li Ch'ing-chao

(TWAS 5)

TWAYNE'S WORLD AUTHORS SERIES (TWAS)

The purpose of TWAS is to survey the major writers —novelists, dramatists, historians, poets, philosophers, and critics—of the nations of the world. Among the national literatures covered are those of Australia, Canada, China, Eastern Europe, France, Germany, Greece, India, Italy, Japan, Latin America, New Zealand, Poland, Russia, Scandinavia, Spain, and the African nations, as well as Hebrew, Yiddish, and Latin Classical literatures. This survey is complemented by Twayne's United States Authors Series and English Authors Series.

The intent of each volume in these series is to present a critical-analytical study of the works of the writer; to include biographical and historical material that may be necessary for understanding, appreciation, and critical appraisal of the writer; and to present all material in clear, concise English—but not to vitiate the scholarly content of the work by doing so.

Li Ch'ing-chao

By HU PIN-CHING

College of Chinese Culture
Republic of China

Twayne Publishers, Inc.   ::   New York

22075

Copyright © 1966 by Twayne Publishers, Inc.

All Rights Reserved

Library of Congress Catalog Card Number: 66–16122

MANUFACTURED IN THE UNITED STATES OF AMERICA

PL2682
.Z5 H8

To Dr. Chang Ch'i-yün,

FOUNDER OF THE COLLEGE OF CHINESE CULTURE

Preface

This book fulfils a twofold aim: to study analytically the complete poetical works of Li Ch'ing-chao in particular and to expose Chinese views on the nature of poetry in general.

Li Ch'ing-chao is the greatest poetess in Chinese literature and a specialist in the art of *tz'u,* poetry for singing. Her works, though not plentiful, have nevertheless exercised great influence on poets of her time and on those of later generations. The present study briefly presents the times as they relate to the poetess' works, considers the origin and evolution of *tz'u,* translates the poetical works of Li Ch'ing-chao, and critically discusses them from various angles: semantic, auditory, grammatical, and conceptual.

While studying the poetical works of Li Ch'ing-chao in particular, the writer applies the method of critical analysis to the features of *tz'u* in general. Therefore, this book is not only a critical-analytical study of Li Ch'ing-chao, but also an introduction to the art of Chinese poetry.

In recent years, a great deal of *shih* (poetry) has been translated into English and French, and there have also been quite a few biographies of individual Chinese poets such as Li Po, Po Chü-I, and others. However, translations of *tz'u* (poetry for singing) have been rare, and little has been written about *tz'u* writers. This circumstance is not surprising since *tz'u* considered only as a branch of *shih,* is more subtle and shaded with nuance; and, consequently, it is less translatable.

In response to the invitation of the editor of Twayne's World Authors Series, I have made an attempt to contribute a study of the great Sung poetess. My task has been rendered extremely difficult by the fact that references to her life are few and that, of the six volumes of *tz'u* written by her, only some fifty pieces have been preserved and handed down to us.

There are poems that lend themselves easily to translation and others that are almost untranslatable. If I had had ample material and had been free to make selections from it, I feel that my translations would be more satisfactory. As this was not the case, I have been obliged to translate indiscriminately all of her *tz'u,* including those that are highly allusive and require exhaustive commentary. Because of these difficulties, I am afraid that the results attained may not be balanced in quality.

I shall consider myself most fortunate if this modest volume finds an echo in the hearts of Western friends of Chinese poetry.

HU PIN-CHING

Contents

Chronology

1083   Birth of Li Ch'ing-chao.

1101   Marriage.

1103   Graduation of her husband from the Imperial Academy.

1114   Date of her portrait.

1122   Appointment of her husband as Magistrate of Laichow.

1126   Appointment of her husband as Magistrate of Tzuch'uan.

1128   Death of her mother-in-law and departure of her husband for Nanking.

1128   Appointment of her husband as Magistrate of Nanking.

1129   Appointment in March of her husband as Magistrate of Huchow.

1129   Death of her husband in August.

1131   Search for refuge in Yungchai, Shaohsin, and Ch'ühsien.

1132   Residence with her brother in Chinhua.

1135   Writing of *Epilogue to a Critical-Analytical Study of Metal and Stone Inscriptions*.

1136   Sending of two poems via peace envoys Hu and Han of the Sung court to the Chin court.

(*Nothing definite can be traced from her fifty-third year onward.*)

CHAPTER 1

Historical Background

I *The Sung Dynasty* (A.D. 960–1279)

THE T'ang dynasty, known as the Golden Age of Chinese Poetry, was brought to an end in 907 A.D. During the succeeding fifty years, the empire was again torn into small pieces. Besides the five dynasties that were considered legitimate and that gave their name to the period, ten smaller individual dynasties were established on the periphery of Central China. These were known as the Ten States.

Unity was re-established in the empire in 960 by the Sung dynasty, which carried out financial, military, and administrative reforms in order to restore the authority of the central government. For more than a hundred and seventy years, the Sung dynasty was characterized by peace and prosperity. In the big cities such as K'aifeng and Loyang, thanks to the development of commerce, people enjoyed a high standard of living. Art and literature, particularly encouraged by the visionary Emperor Hui-tsung, flourished under his reign. Emperor Hui-tsung was not only a patron of art and literature but also a poet, musician, and painter of no mean skill. It was he who founded the Academy of Painting, in which the candidates who applied for admission had to participate in a contest that consisted of painting a picture to illustrate a given verse. One of these verses has remained famous to this day: "Treading upon fallen petals on its way home,/the horse has perfumed hoofs." The artist painted a horse followed by a swarm of butterflies.

However, this romantic Emperor did not concern himself much with affairs of state but indulged in luxury, pleasure, revelry, and dissipation. The second stanza of a *tz'u* written by him reflects well the atmosphere of extravagance that reigned in his court.

Every household is celebrating peace.
Roads strewn with flowers,

The moon following the nightly songsters.
In the Dragon Pavilion, a jade lamp is seen glistening.
The flutes sound indistinct;
The feast is being served in the elevated realm of P'eng-
  Ying.*

His love of pleasure and growing extravagance led to an invasion by the Chin, a barbarous tribe from the north, which resulted in the downfall of the Northern Sung dynasty. Hui-tsung and his son, Emperor Ch'in-tsung, in whose favor he abdicated, were taken prisoner. The Sung were then obliged to take refuge on the south bank of the Yangtze River. In 1128, a member of the imperial household moved the capital to the city of Hangchow in Chekiang and established the Southern Sung dynasty, as distinguished from the Northern Sung dynasty, which had its capital in K'aifeng, Honan.

Nevertheless, the Southern Sung dynasty, after having made peace with the Chin, still enjoyed comparative security and prosperity, as shown by these poetic lines:

South of the river, gentlemen still retain
The gallantry of the periods of Hsüan Ho and Cheng Ho.†
Green casements, vermilion gates,
Hooks of silver shining for miles and miles.

As the élite of the nation had gone with the court to Hangchow, art and literature continued to flourish, and intellectual pursuits regained the same splendor in South China as in past days. The fanciful Emperor Hui-tsung concerned himself with art and literature as much as had Emperor Hsüan-tsung of the T'ang.

Under the reign of Emperor Hui-tsung, an atmosphere of luxury and dissipation prevailed not only in his court but also among the courtiers and men of letters, who rivaled him in extravagance. They occupied themselves with daily excursions and nightly revelry, feasting and surrounding themselves with singing girls and famous courtesans, on whose lips verses in praise of life and love were commonplace.

They sang in praise of the emperor:

* The imperial abode is so full of joy that it is likened to the fairyland of P'englai and Yingchow.
† Era names during the reign of Emperor Hui-tsung.

In the Jade Palace, the immortals are feasting.
Leaf after leaf,
Peach blossoms are swept down to earth by the
                               wind of late spring.
Across the emerald clouds,
Wheels of gold chariots are heard indistinctly rolling.

The beauties of the thirty-six harems
Are richly painted and perfumed,
The Jade Palace of Tz'u Ning is celebrating
                           the flowers in bloom.
On this beauteous night, a thousand candles
Reflect the bloom of youth.

They sang in praise of the leisure class:

      Talented men and *tz'u* writers
      Are comparable to prime ministers clad in white.
      Fain would I give up vain glory
      For a cup of wine and a whispered song.

      Awakening from tipsiness,
      Whither am I?
      On a river bank surrounded by willows,
      In the morning wind, under a sinking moon.

They sang love songs:

On horseback amidst perfumed dust,
I met Lady Hsieh on a road south of the city.
Without make-up, her loveliness still reigned supreme.
A thousand charms are born in a smile.

Her cloudy hair meets the crescent-shaped eyebrows,
The redness of wine mounts on her rainbow-colored cheeks.
Awakening from her spring dream, the sun is already
                         slanting to the west.

They sang in praise of country life:

          Beauteous is the south bank:
          Aquatic villages, fishing ports,
          A trail of smoke, solitary and fine.

In a word, their songs reflect the full blissfulness of life and constitute the poetry called *tz'u*, which flourished under the Sung.

II   *The Evolution of Chinese Poetry*

Before describing the poetic works of Li Ch'ing-chao, it is necessary to touch upon the evolution of Chinese poetry and the kind of poetry representative of the Sung period. Chinese poetry dates back to the earliest recorded Chinese history, and its fixed verse forms are multiple and varied. But prior to the T'ang, there were no fixed verse forms. The number of syllables in a line and the number of lines in a poem were indefinite. There was neither fixed tone pattern nor invariable rhyme scheme. The first Chinese poem, *The Song of Lady T'u Shan*—supposed to be authentic and cited in the *Annals of the Spring and Autumn Period*—has only two verses, the first of which is trisyllabic and the second monosyllabic. Since Chinese characters are monosyllabic, in poetry the number of syllables in each line is identical with the number of characters.

The Book of Odes (about twelfth to seventh centuries B.C.), the first anthology of Chinese poetry, contains poems usually written in four-syllabic lines, with occasional lines of more or fewer syllables. The poems are usually divided into short stanzas. In *The Poems of Ch'u*, the second anthology of Chinese poetry, consisting of poems written by Ch'ü Yüan (322–295 B.C.) and his disciple Sung Yü, the poems are mostly in lines of seven syllables with occasional lines of nine syllables. *The Poems of Ch'u* are interminably long, and there are pauses in nearly each line. In the seven-syllabic verse the pause, marked by the non-semantic word *hsi*, comes after the third syllable; that in the nine-syllabic verse comes after the fourth syllable.

Regular seven-syllabic and five-syllabic verse first appeared in Chinese poetry under the Han dynasty. The first Chinese poem in seven-syllabic meter was composed collectively by Emperor Wu (141–87 B.C.) of the Western Han dynasty and twenty-five courtiers. The five-word meter was introduced from the non-Chinese by Mei Ch'eng, a contemporary of the Emperor. The poems, written in lines of seven or five syllables with neither fixed tone pattern nor fixed number of lines, are known as "ancient verse," as distinguished from the regulated verses with uniform structure. In ancient verse, the number of lines in a poem is indefinite, but the number of syllables in each line, as I have said, is limited to either seven or five. Rhyme occurs at the end of the even-numbered lines, and one can either use one rhyme throughout or vary it, as one wishes.

During the T'ang dynasty, the form of poetry came to be definitely fixed, with a more uniform structure arrangement. Two types of poem with fixed forms came into being: the eight-line poem and the quatrain. In an eight-line poem, all the lines must be either five-syllabic or seven-syllabic; the same rhyme is used throughout the poem, and it occurs at the end of the even-numbered verses, rhyming at the end of the first line being optional. The four lines in the middle must form two antithetic couplets. There is a fixed tone pattern, since variation in tone plays an important part in Chinese prosody.

As Chinese is a tonal language, each character is pronounced in a fixed tone. The division of tones varies according to different localities, but in classical Chinese there are four tones; the first is known as "flat" (*p'ing sheng*); the other three, as "sharps" (*che sheng*). These tones differ from each other not only in pitch but also in length and movement. The first tone is relatively long and keeps to the same pitch, whereas the other three are comparatively short, with upward or downward modulation.

The quatrain metrically corresponds to half of an eight-line poem in regulated verse, with the difference being that there is no obligatory antithetical couplet. Under the T'ang, poems were variously composed on the model of the eight-line poem, the quatrain, and the ancient verse. Toward the end of the dynasty, another kind of poetry known as *tz'u,* or poetry adapted to a given melody, was developed. The word *tz'u* means "words for singing" and is used to denote poetry in lines of unequal length, written to existing music, as differentiated from the ordinary poetry in lines of equal length described previously.

Famous poems in the T'ang were sometimes adapted to tunes and sung by talented courtesans, the adaptations being done by musicians. However, in writing a *tz'u,* the poet chooses a tune or composes one himself and then writes words for it. A poem so written bears no title but the name of the tune. As every tune has an original song, which has a separate tone pattern and rhyme scheme of its own, the structure of a *tz'u* adapted to a given tune is determined by that of the original song, its model. There are a total of about seven or eight hundred models, each with its particular name.

Various *tz'u* written on the same model bear the generic name that denotes the tune and the original song, and should have the same structure as the model. Unlike ordinary poems, usually composed of verses of equal length, poems adapted to music are generally composed of verses of different length; but the number of syllables in each line is fixed. The rules of versification in *tz'u* are more complicated than those governing ordinary poetry because, in writing an ordinary poem, the poet has but to distinguish flats from sharps; in writing a *tz'u*, he has also to bear in mind the fact that the flat tone (*p'ing sheng*) is subdivided into two, *yin p'ing* and *yang p'ing;* and the sharp tone (*che sheng*) is subdivided into three: *shang sheng* (mounting tone), *ch'ü sheng* (parting tone), and *ju sheng* (entering tone). In other words, in writing a *tz'u*, the poet is not only obliged to follow the rules governing the arrangement of flats and sharps, but also the arrangement of subtones in each of the constituent lines. Thus, a poet who writes a *tz'u* adapted to the given melody, *As in a Dream*, must follow strictly the rules governing the length of each constituent line, the rhyme scheme, and the arrangement of subtones, though some liberty is allowed with regard to the latter.

For instance, the model *As in a Dream* is composed of six lines, the first of which comprises six characters; the second, six; the third, five; the fourth, five; the fifth, four (but consisting of a two-word repetition), the sixth, six. The length of the constituent lines, the arrangement of tones and the rhyme scheme of a *tz'u* by Li Ch'ing-chao modeled on *As in a Dream* are given in the example below, with numbers representing different subtones, and with R denoting the rhyme, accompanied by the romanization and translation of the original text.

Tso yeh yü su feng tsou   R
5   4   3   1   1   4

Nung shui pu hsiao ch'ien chiu   R
2   4   1   1   3   3

Shih wen chüan lien jen
4   4   3   2   2

Ch'üeh tao hai t'ang yi chiu   R
5   4   3   2   1   4

Chih fou chin fou   R
1   3   1   3

Yin shih lu fei hung shou   R
1   4   5   2   2   4

Last night, the rain was fine, the wind sudden.
A heavy slumber did not dissipate my tipsiness.
I ask the one who rolls up the screen how the begonias are.
She says they are as of yore.
Know you not? Know you not?
'Tis time when the green should be fat and the red thin.

This kind of poetry, or *tz'u,* which first appeared toward the end
of the T'ang dynasty and marked the beginning of a new era for
Chinese poetry, became widespread during the Five Dynasty period. Literary activities were then concentrated in the Kingdom
of Shu, located in Szechwan, and in the Kingdom of Southern
T'ang, by the southern bank of the Yangtze River. It was in the
Kingdom of Shu that an anthology of *tz'u* entitled *Among the
Flowers* was compiled, but it was limited to the works of those
poets who had lived and written in that kingdom. As the mood
in these small states was one of luxury amidst insecurity, sover-
eigns and courtiers were carefree and forgot their sorrows by
indulging in drinking and pleasure. Consequently, the *tz'u* writers
of the Five Dynasty period had the same inspiration: they used
beautiful words in praise of wine, women, and voluptuousness.
They had the same style: their language was refined, flowery,
and sumptuous. On the whole, their works accurately reflect the
dissipated court life of that period.

Tz'u was carried to great perfection under the Sung. While the
tz'u of the preceding period was empty and artificial, that of the
Sung was characterized by simplicity, sobriety, and sincerity.
After the Sung moved their capital to Hangchow, great *tz'u* writers such as Hsin Ch'i-chi and Lu yu composed powerful verses
to celebrate patriotism. Thus, *tz'u* was no longer a mere amuse-
ment for men of letters but a powerful instrument for expressing
noble sentiment.

There are two kinds of *tz'u: hsiao ling* (small tunes) and *man
tz'u* (slow tunes). The latter was created from 1034 onward and
was written to be adapted to newly composed melodies. By that
time, *tz'u* had definitely come into vogue. It was sung in court,
at meetings of men of letters, on festival days, or on parting with
a friend. After the fall of the T'ang, poetry suffered a decline.
When a literary form has been widely employed but unchanged

for a long time, it naturally becomes hackneyed. An original poet, who will be reluctant to say the same things over and over again in the same manner, will discover new forms to show originality and independence. This is why poetry changes from age to age. The Chinese poetry that had reached the zenith of glory under the T'ang was replaced by *tz'u* under the Sung.

III   *The Origin of* tz'u; *Its Special Characteristics*

As to the origin of *tz'u*, what Chang Huei-yen has said is both simple and clear. In his preface to *Selections of Tz'u*, he wrote: "*Tz'u* originated with the T'ang poets who set poems to the tunes of Yüeh Fu (The Department of Music). When poems are set to music, they become words for singing. That is why poems for singing are called *tz'u*, which means 'the words of a song.'"

As T'ang poems were composed of equal length, they could not be adapted in their existing form to musical phrases, which were usually unequal in length. Consequently, when poems were adapted to tunes, one was obliged to add words void of meaning in order to fit the tunes. As this was most unsatisfactory, poets, at the request of the musicians or at their own discretion, began to write poems corresponding to the structure of the tunes to make their poetry suitable for singing. This is how *tz'u* first came into being.

I have already mentioned that there are two kinds of *tz'u*: *hsiao ling* and *man tz'u*. During the late T'ang, the Five Dynasty, and the Northern Sung periods, there was only *hsiao ling;* this resembled *shih* very much in structure. For instance, the tune *Sheng Ch'a T'zu* is like two five-syllabic quatrains with a sharp rhyme. The tune *Spring in the Jade Pavilion* is like two seven-syllabic quatrains with a sharp rhyme; the tune *Partridges in the Sky* is like two seven-syllabic quatrains with a flat rhyme.

It was under the reign of Jen-tsung of the Northern Sung that *man tz'u* was created. Such poets as Chou Pang-yen, Wan-szu Ya-yen, and Chiang K'uei, who were excellent musicians, composed new tunes that were much longer, more complicated, and more varied in structure than the earlier *hsiao ling.* Consequently, *tz'u* modeled on these new tunes is longer and more complicated in construction than that adapted to ancient tunes, and the rules governing the arrangement of tones in *man tz'u* are much stricter than those in *hsiao ling.* In the latter, the poet is allowed some liberty with regard to the arrangement of subtones; in the former, the poet has to observe very strictly the rules governing the arrangement of the five subtones: *yin p'ing, yang p'ing, shang sheng, ch'ü sheng,* and *ju sheng.*

In this connection, an anecdote may be cited. The father of Chang Yen once composed a verse which first read as follows: "The swastika-adorned window is deep." When set to music, it did not sound well, so he changed it to: "The swastika-adorned window is dark." This did not sound well on the flute either, so he finally changed it into: "The swastika-adorned window is bright." The words "deep" (*shen*), "dark" (*yin*), and "bright" (*ming*) all belong to the group of flats (*p'ing sheng*); but the word "bright" belongs to the group of *yang p'ing,* while the other two belong to that of *yin p'ing.* That is why only the word "bright" is harmonious, and the other two are not. As the word "bright" and the word "dark" are opposed in sense, it shows that a poet sometimes sacrifices sincerity to form. Of course, a poet more skilful than the father of Chang Yen would be able to find the right word without this sacrifice.

Tz'u differs from *shih* not only in form but also in essence. All human beings have feelings. When feelings are put down on paper, they become prose. But prose is only proper for expressing ordinary feelings and is inadequate to express more subtle and delicate sentiments. Consequently, poetry is created to describe what cannot be expressed by prose. When poetry proves to be insufficient to express sentiments still more delicate, more vague, and with greater nuance, *tz'u* is created to depict what poetry cannot.

At the very beginning, poets made only slight changes in their poems so as to fit them into tunes. For this reason the *tz'u* of Po Chü-I and Liu Yü-hsi was not very different from their *shih,* either in form or essence. Toward the end of the T'ang, new discoveries were made in the domain of *tz'u,* with such poets as Wen T'ing-yün and Wei Chuang proving to be excellent *tz'u* writers:

Modeled on *Clepsydra*

A jade burner with incense,
A red candle in tears
Reflect purposely autumn thoughts in the painted hall.
Her cloudy hair is disheveled,
Her quilt and pillow are chilled in the lengthy night.

The plane tree
And the midnight rain
Are indifferent to the bitter sorrow of parted lovers.
Leaf after leaf,
Drop after drop,
They fall on the empty perrons till dawn.

Modeled on *The Cup of the Lotus Leaf*

I still recall that year, under the flowers,
Late at night,
When I first met Lady Hsieh.
West of the aquatic pavilion with painted screens drooping,
Hand in hand, we secretly hoped to meet again.

Over the morning oriole and the sinking moon we fretted
And we parted.
Since then we are separated without news.
Today, each of us being in a different land,
How can we expect to meet again?

The two pieces of *tz'u* cited were written by Wen T'ing-yün and Wei Chuang, respectively; and the poetic world in them differs from that in their *shih*. If *tz'u* had not existed by that time, they would not have been able to express such sentiments. Chinese poetry attained its highest glory in the middle of the T'ang, and it was only natural that it should change its form towards the end of the dynasty, just as an overflowing river changes its bed to form new waterways.

Generally speaking, *tz'u* belongs to the family of *shih*; but, if we want to be precise, it differs from *shih* in these ways: both seek to express sentiment by means of images and symbols, but the images and symbols in *tz'u* are more subtle and delicate than those found in *shih*. For instance, in *tz'u*, when referring to natural phenomena, the poet uses such expressions as "fine rain," "pale moon," and "rare stars." When describing a landscape, he employs such expressions as "distant hills" and "meandering streams." In depicting plants, he speaks of "flying catkins" and "drooping willows." In describing articles of daily use, he speaks of "silver lamps" and "jade incense burners." In describing feelings, he speaks of "idle worries" and "intimate thoughts." "Colored sleeves" and "silk robes" refer to clothing; "emerald screens" and "tortoise beams" to interior decoration. In *tz'u*, the halls are always "painted," the balustrades are "sculptured," the willows are "gloomy," the flowers are "obscure." Willows and flowers are only objects; but, if one speaks of "gloomy willows" and "obscure flowers," a different kind of world is created.

Of course, such epithets are also used in ordinary poetry, but where they are considered too dainty for ordinary poetry, they are indispensable in *tz'u* because, in writing *tz'u*, the poet should always refer to dainty objects to indicate delicacy. Even in *tz'u* expressing noble and sublime sentiments such as patriotism, tiny objects are also cited. For instance, in a *tz'u* written after the invasion of the Chin tribes, Chiang K'uei wrote:

After the barbarous horses peep at the river,
Even the abandoned pools and the tall trees are tired of war.
The evening horns are heard in an empty city.

. . . .

The twenty-four bridges are still here.
Waves are agitated,
The cold moon is soundless.

In another *tz'u* devoted to the same theme, he wrote: "Alas! Mountains and rivers/Echo only the song of the cuckoo."

Even Hsin Ch'i-chi, a well-known *tz'u* writer of the Sung who had a powerful style, expressed sentiments of woe by means of tiny objects:

Dance not!
See you not Yü Huan and Fei Yen turned into dust?*
Idle worries are the bitterest of all.
Lean not against the dangerous balustrade;
The sinking sun is there.
Heart-rending is the hazy willow.

As a perfect example of the characteristics of *tz'u*, I cite a *tz'u* by Ch'in Kuan, modeled on *Washing Brook Sand:*

A vast stretch of coolness mounts the small pavilion.
Morning gloominess evokes late autumn.
On the painted screen, pale mist, flowing stream.

* Two historical beauties.

Flying petals are as free and light as dreams,
Skeins of rain are as fine as those of sorrows.
Small hooks of silver idly hang my precious curtains.

This *tz'u* is a fusion of scene and emotion. The poetic world is composed of a small pavilion wherein are found such dainty objects as precious curtains hung on small hooks of silver and a painted screen on which are drawn a flowing stream and a thin layer of mist. "Morning gloominess" and "coolness" are used to denote time. Outside the small pavilion, flying petals are "as light as dreams," and skeins of rain are "as fine as skeins of sorrow." Each expression is delicately elaborated and finely wrought. The special function of *tz'u* is to create a poetic world by means of dainty objects endowed with suggestive power.

There is a certain airiness about *tz'u* that is not found in ordinary poetry, a lightness that does not however imply shallowness or frivolity. Even *tz'u*, expressing profound thought and sublime emotion, still retains that airy character. Let us now study and compare a *shih* and a *tz'u*.

This eight-line poem (a *shih*) was written by the great T'ang poet Tu Fu upon his return from lengthy exile. The atmosphere in Chinese is sad and heavy.

Astonished by my presence,
Once the surprise is over,
My wife and children dry their tears.
In times of trouble, returning alive from a long exile
     is haphazard.
Peeping beyond the wall,
My neighbors are moved to sobs and sighs.
Late at night, under the candlelight,
Facing one another,
We still believe 'tis only a dream.

These lines are the second stanza of a *tz'u* by Yen Chi-tao, celebrating reunion with his lady love. The theme is similar to that of Tu Fu, but what difference in style! One is heavy as stone, the other light as a feather.

Since your departure,
Longing for the hour of reunion,

> Myriad times have I dreamed of you.
> Tonight, under the glistening lamp of silver,
> I still fear that we are meeting in a dream.

Tz'u is very limited in inspiration. Prose or ordinary poetry can be used to describe scenes or emotion, and also as a means of reasoning and arguing. The function of *tz'u*, however, is limited to describing scenes and expressing emotion. If a poet tries to incorporate argument into *tz'u*, his writing looks affected and artificial. For instance, Hsin Ch'i-chi, who found ample scope in *tz'u*, still failed in using it for purposes of argumentation:

> Fame as vain as the shell of a snail,
> Profit as small as the head of a fly,
> Why should we busy ourselves with them?
> Weakness or power,
> Everything is predestined,
> While my idle body has not yet aged.
> Set me free,
> Let me be lazy and crazy.
> If I live to a hundred years,
> Let me get drunk
> During thirty-six thousand days.

When we read this *tz'u*, how tasteless and void of flavor it seems! This is effective evidence that *tz'u* should not be employed to further an argument. Thus we see that *tz'u* differs from *shih* not only in form but also in essence. Although *tz'u* is derived from *shih*, it is more limited in inspiration. *Tz'u* is purely lyric and is not suitable for reasoning or arguing. Although ordinary poetry may be used as a means of edifying or moralizing, the function of *tz'u* is limited to the description of scenes and the expression of emotions. This limitation of inspiration is due to the fact that a *tz'u* is a song, and the function of a song is essentially to sing and to move the heart. In other words, it must be lyric.

The poetic world in *tz'u* can be likened to a landscape wrapped in a thin layer of mist or a flower seen in the moonlight. It is at once far and near, real and unreal, existent and non-existent. The reason *tz'u* arose is that this kind of poetry corresponds exactly to certain natural scenery and human sentiment. So long as such scenery and sentiment exist, *tz'u* will also last and find its way into our hearts. Where natural phenomena are concerned, oblique wind, fine rain, and thin mist constitute a perfect world for *tz'u*. Where landscape is concerned, smooth lakes, distant hills, and meandering streams constitute an ideal world for *tz'u*. Where human sentiment is concerned, languor, idleness, longing, and regret constitute a real world for *tz'u*.

A genuine *tz'u* writer must be rich in sensitivity, pure in nature, tender in heart, and free in spirit. Li Ch'ing-chao had these qualities; she was a genuine *tz'u* writer. Unfortunately, of the six volumes of *tz'u* written by her, only some fifty pieces, as I have previously indicated, assembled in a volume entitled *Tz'u of Pure Jade* have been preserved and handed down to us.

CHAPTER 2

The Life of Li Ch'ing-chao

I   The Position of Women in Ancient China

I WANT to say at the outset that in ancient China a severe distinction was drawn between the sexes. A poem from *The Book of Odes* tells us that when sons were born, they slept on couches, clothed in splendid robes, and had jade scepters with which to play. When daughters were born, they were put to sleep on the ground, clothed in wrappers, and had tiles with which to play. Girls were supposed to do neither wrong nor good; they were to think only about embroidery and cooking. They were not supposed to interfere in matters that did not lie within these spheres.

Thus, in ancient China, men belonged to the privileged class, while women were deprived even of the right of education. Chinese women were either illiterate or limited in learning to the studying of *The Book on Virtuous Women*. They enjoyed no freedom of thought, no freedom of action, no freedom of love, and no freedom of expression. Physically, from about the tenth century onward, they were handicapped by bound feet, which confined them to the inner apartments. A woman's virtue consisted chiefly in obedience. Unmarried, she owed obedience to her father; married, to her husband; in widowhood, to her sons.

There was a time-honored and well-known proverb concerning the fair sex: "A woman's virtue lies in her ignorance." That is why, in spite of China's ancient civilization and her long history, prominent woman writers were few and far between. In fact, women rarely appeared in Chinese literature. The Han dynasty, which lasted four hundred years, counted only two outstanding women writers. There was Pan Chao, a sister of the great historian Pan Ku, who helped her brother to complete the history of the Han. There was also Ts'ai Wen-chi, a Chinese girl who was taken prisoner by the barbarians. She married one of them; bore him two sons; and, upon her return after a twelve-year exile, wrote a long narrative poem entitled *The Song of Chagrin and*

Indignation. The T'ang dynasty had thousands of poets, but only two poetesses of the T'ang are well remembered: Hsüeh T'ao and Yü Hsüan-chi. Hsüeh T'ao was a famous courtesan, while Yü Hsüan-chi was a romantic nun. Although some of their poems have been handed down to us, their literary achievements are far from comparable to those of Li Po, Tu Fu, or Po Chü-i.

The only woman whose literary fame was not eclipsed by that of men was Li Ch'ing-chao, the great woman *tz'u* writer of the Sung. She was a genius, an epoch-making poetess who was on an equal footing with her contemporaries in prosody, rhetoric, and creation. The sobriety of her language, the harmony of her verses, the originality of her poetic imagery, and the sincerity of her emotion contributed to the perfection of her style. Therefore, it is no exaggeration to say that Li Ch'ing-chao is not only a great *tz'u* writer of the Sung dynasty, but also the greatest poetess of Chinese literature.

II *The Childhood of Li Ch'ing-chao*

Li Ch'ing-chao, China's greatest poetess, was born in 1083 in Shantung Province, China, during the reign of Emperor Shen-tsung. The place where she was born was called, appropriately, "Willow Flower Fountain." The prefecture of Chinan is also called the "City of Fountains" because it contains seventy-two fountains abounding in lotus flowers and surrounded by willows. In this regard, the famous Ch'ing novelist Liu Ngo wrote:

> When one enters the city of Chinan, one
> will soon notice that there is a fountain in
> every house and willows in front of every door.

Of all the fountains in Chinan, the Po-t'u Fountain is the largest. In that fountain, there are three natural water spouts, which reach a height of two feet. The water of the fountain is as blue as sapphire and as limpid as crystal, and the fountain itself is rectangular, surrounded by willows with which are mingled cherry, peach, and pomegranate blossoms.

Not far from Po-t'u Fountain are Jade Fountain and Willow Flower Fountain, both enclosed by stone balustrades. Only fish are allowed to swim in their blue waves. The fountains are covered with the green foliage and red flowers of the river bank, in the luxuriance of which songs of birds respond to the gurgling waters.

Near the Pure Jade Fountain and the Willow Flower Fountain is said to be the ancient abode of poetess Li Ch'ing-chao. It is an old-style house, composed of three rooms. Biographical works about her and her poetry are there on exhibition. A portrait that hangs on the wall, showing her with a branch of chrysanthemums in her hand, is said to have been painted by a Ch'ing artist of the Ch'ien-lung era (1736–95).

As Li Ch'ing-chao loved chrysanthemums, to which she often likened herself, yellow chrysanthemums in her memory are planted near the house. It is most likely that the Pure Jade Fountain derived its name from her collection of *tz'u*.

Li Ch'ing-chao began life under favorable circumstances. Her father, Li Ko-fei, Minister of Rites, was a well-known prose writer. His essay, *The Gardens of Loyang*, was highly esteemed by Sung poet Su Tung-po. Her mother, a granddaughter of scholar Wang Kung-ch'en, also wrote poems and essays. As her parents were highly cultured, Li Ch'ing-chao in early childhood received from them a good education, quite contrary to the time-honored tradition that deprived women of the right to learn. From adolescence, she had a strong predilection for the creation of poetry. Two verses written in early youth are illustrative of this:

> The creative impulse makes me restless as a
> nocturnal bird
> Reluctant to perch after flying three
> rounds.

High birth, good education, and natural gifts combined to make her the greatest poetess that Chinese history has ever known.

III *The Married Life of Li Ch'ing-chao*

Time flies like an arrow, as the Chinese proverb says, and our young poetess quickly ripened into womanhood. At eighteen she married Chao Ming-ch'eng, a student of the Imperial Academy and a well-known epigraphist. He was a native of Chu-ch'eng in Shantung Province. His father, Chao T'ing-chin, who later became Prime Minister, was then Minister of Interior.

There was a legend about her marriage with Chao Ming-ch'eng. In his teens, Chao Ming-ch'eng once dreamed of a strange book. Awakened, he remembered only three sentences from it: 1. The word *yen* (speech) and the word *szu* (in charge of) combine to make a single word. 2. The upper part of the word *an* (peace) is gone. 3. The word *chih* (orchid) and the word *fu* (hibiscus) are stripped of the word *ts'ao* (grass).

Deeply intrigued, Chao Ming-ch'eng told his father about the puzzling dream. As the father was expert in explaining dreams, he said to his son:

"My child, you will probably marry a poetess some day. I shall tell you why. The third sentence corresponds to the words 'the husband of,' because the word *fu* (hibiscus) is composed of the words *ts'ao* (grass) and *fu* (husband). When stripped of the word *ts'ao* (grass), the word *fu* (hibiscus) becomes the word *fu* (husband). On the other hand, the word *chih* (orchid) is composed of the words *ts'ao* (grass) and *chih* (of). When stripped of the word *ts'ao*, the word *chih* (orchid) becomes the word *chih* (of). Therefore, the third sentence corresponds to these words: 'the husband of.'

"Of whom? Let us see. The second sentence corresponds to the word 'woman' because the word *an* (peace) is comprised of two parts: the upper part is a sign representing a roof, while the lower part is the word *nü* (woman). When the upper part is gone, the word *an* (peace) becomes the word *nü* (woman).

"The first sentence corresponds to the word *tz'u* (poetry for singing), because the word *tz'u* is composed of the word *yen* (speech) and the word *szu* (in charge of).

"Therefore, the three sentences from the book you dreamed of correspond to these words: 'the husband of a woman specialized in the art of *tz'u*.'"

This strange dream actually came true when Li Ko-fei married his daughter to Chao Ming-ch'eng; the bridegroom was then twenty-one years old.

The highly cultured young couple loved each other deeply and lived in perfect harmony. The following poem, written by Li Ch'ing-chao shortly after her marriage, reflects the blissfulness of her married life.

Modeled on *Magnolia*

From a strolling peddler
I bought a branch of spring blossoms

Whose rosy cheeks
Are still loaded with the tears of dew-drops.

Lest my beloved should say,
Your face is less fair than the flowers,
I stuck them aslant in my cloudlike tresses
So that he could compare.

The foregoing *tz'u* is tender, delicate, and natural, full of coquetry and charm. It depicts perfectly the young bride's state of
mind.

In the first stanza, the comparison of spring blossoms loaded
with dew-drops to rosy cheeks stained with tears is ingenious.

As he was still a student, Chao Ming-ch'eng had to absent himself frequently from home. Alone in her chamber, Li Ch'ing-chao
wrote a most exquisite poem to express longing for her beloved,
and copied it on a silk handkerchief, which she sent him.

Modeled on *A Bouquet of Plum Flowers*

The scent of red lotus is gone, autumn is on the jade mat.
Slightly slackening my belt,
Alone I step into a boat.
Who sends me a brocade message from the clouds?
When the wild geese return, in formation,
The west pavilion is full of moonbeams.

Alone the flowers fade, alone the water flows.
One kind of longing,
Idle worries in two places.
How to get rid of these feelings?
Hardly having left my eyebrows,
They creep into my heart.

Indeed, autumn is a cruel season. Faded flowers, chilliness, and
wild geese whining and groaning combine to create an atmosphere of desolation. The wild geese flying in formation usually
depict a figure resembling the Chinese character *i* (one) or *jen*
(man.) Consequently, they are suggestive of messages from the
clouds, evocative of the change in season, the passing of time,
and the delayed return of the loved one. Therefore, they remind
the poetess of the absent husband whom she does not forget.

"Alone the flowers fade, alone the water flows." In these simple lines is hidden a profound meaning. The poetess watches the faded blossoms. They wither alone, their perfume is gone. Yet who pities them? Flowers are likened to youth. Youth is short-lived, as fleeting as the flowers. As she is boating, she stares at the water flowing by. Water also has a symbolic value, representing time. Time is like a flowing river, a river of no return.

In the last two lines, sad feelings are personified so as to produce a striking effect. When she frowns, it is Sadness who mounts her eyebrows. When she stops frowning, it is Sadness, invisible but always present, who quits the eyebrows only to creep into her heart.

On the first and fifteenth of each month, Chao Ming-ch'eng was granted leave of absence from school. As the Chao family was not rich, the young student on his way home used to pawn his clothes for five hundred copper coins in order to buy some fruit and reproductions of stone inscriptions at Hsiang-kuo Temple. The husband and wife savored the fruit and enjoyed studying the reproductions. They likened themselves to the subjects of a legendary emperor, whose attitude toward life was one of contented detachment.

Two years after his marriage, Chao Ming-ch'eng graduated from the Imperial Academy and became a public functionary in the administration. The young couple contented themselves with frugal meals and clothing and spent all their money in buying ancient books and calligraphical works. Their sole ambition was to collect all the rare paintings, calligraphical works, and antiques that could be found. When his meager salary did not allow him such extravagances, Chao Ming-ch'eng still, as during his school days, had to sell his garments or personal belongings to satisfy his whims. As Chao Ming-ch'eng's father and many of his relatives and friends worked in the capital, they possessed many rare books, which the young couple borrowed and painstakingly copied.

One day, someone brought them a painting of peonies by Hsü Hsi, a famous painter of flowers and birds of the Five Dynasty period, and asked for twenty thousand copper coins. For want of the required sum, they kept the picture overnight and had to return it to the owner the following day. But they regretted for weeks their inability to purchase the painting.

For ten years, they stayed in their native province, where Chao Ming-ch'eng was magistrate in Laichow and Ch'ingchow, successively. Their savings were spent in buying books and antiques. Whenever a new book was added to their collection, they busied themselves with reading, correcting, and cataloguing. Whenever paintings or calligraphical works were bought, they rolled and unrolled the scrolls time and again. Whenever an ancient wine pot was acquired, they examined it with great attention. They corrected the mistakes in the books, pointed out the faults in the antiques, and limited the time of appreciation to the burning of one candle. Every evening, after dinner, they sat together and played a game they had invented for themselves. They poured a cup of tea and seated themselves in front of a pile of books. The game consisted of pointing out in which volume, on which page, and in which line such or such an event was mentioned. The one who guessed correctly was the winner and had the privilege of taking a sip of the jasmine tea. Sometimes they enjoyed themselves so immensely and laughed so much that they caused the tea cup to tumble from their laps. Li Ch'ing-chao had quickly become addicted to her husband's hobby, that of collecting antiques, and proved to be a very helpful mate who astonished her husband by her erudition and prodigious memory.

When the collection of books was completed, they had enormous cabinets made for them. The books were read, corrected, annotated, and catalogued. In order to devote herself fully to these tasks, Li Ch'ing-chao did less cooking, contented herself with simple clothing, deprived herself of pearl and jade ornaments, and neglected embroidery. Everything was spent in buying classics, history books, and antiquities.

By that time, they had also collected a large quantity of ancient objects in bronze and reproductions of inscriptions on steles. Here a remark should be made regarding inscriptions. It seems to have been customary in ancient China to engrave inscriptions, poetic or prosaic, on all sorts of everyday articles, on sacrificial vases, and on funeral and memorial steles. For instance, on an old metal mirror might be found an inscription such as this:

> Man mirrors his face every morning,
> Why not his heart?

By that time, Li Ch'ing-chao and her husband had also begun to write a book entitled *Chin Shih Lu* (*Critical-Analytical Studies of Metal and Stone Inscriptions*). The word *chin* (metal) de-

notes ancient objects in bronze such as ritual vases, incense burners, rice pots, water pots, wine pots, and goblets. The word *shih*
(stone) denotes funeral and memorial steles. Upon ancient bronze
objects and stone steles are usually found inscriptions recording
historical events or praising kings, generals, or other well-known
personalities. By studying these inscriptions, we can obtain much
knowledge of ancient social and political institutions, and can
trace the evolution of Chinese characters.

As Chao Ming-ch'eng was a great collector of antiques and a
famous epigraphist, he studied attentively the inscriptions on
bronze or stone, made criticisms and selections, and compiled
them into a book consisting of thirty volumes. This was the *Chin
Shih Lu,* the critical-analytical study of the inscriptions that had
appeared on two thousand pieces of bronze objects and stone
steles. This book, written by Chao Ming-ch'eng and Li Ch'ing-
chao, is a monumental work.

At the age of thirty-one, Li Ch'ing-chao had her portrait done
by a famous painter. Her cloudlike coiffure, her slim figure, and
her delicate hand holding a branch of chrysanthemums well remind us of many of the poems in which she depicts herself. In
celebration of her birthday, Chao Ming-ch'eng wrote this dedica-
tion on the upper corner of her portrait:

> To Poetess I-an on the Occasion of Her
> Thirty-first Birthday Anniversary:
>
> Her poetry is pure and elegant,
> Her person modest and dignified,
> A real companion for me
>   In my retirement.

In 1126, under the reign of Emperor Ch'in-tsung, Chao Ming-
ch'eng was appointed Magistrate of Tzu-ch'uan in Shantung.
Having heard that the Chin were invading the capital, he looked
regretfully at his numerous trunks full of books and antiques,
knowing that they were not vouchsafed him for long.

In 1127, the first year of the reign of Emperor Kao-tsung of
the Southern Sung, Chao Ming-ch'eng's mother died and he left
alone for Nanking to attend the funeral. As he could not take
with him all he owned, he left behind the heavy volumes, the
ancient bronze objects without epigraphs, the duplicates of paint-

ings and the pictures of no great value, but took with him fifteen cartloads of books. The rest of their possessions were left in the house in Ch'ingchow, where Li Ch'ing-chao stayed alone for some time before joining her husband in Nanking. When the Chin took Ch'ingchow at the end of the year, ten rooms of books were burned to ashes.

Li Ch'ing-chao was then forty-seven years old. While alone in Ch'ingchow, she learned that her father had fallen into disgrace with the emperor. At the same time, homesick and longing for her husband, she wrote two poems to express her mournful thoughts:

End of Spring

Why so homesick at the end of spring?
In illness, my hair seems too long to be combed.
The chattering swallows stay all day long on the beams;
When the gentle breeze sweeps by, rose-scented is my screen.

This is not a *tz'u* but an ordinary poem, a quatrain composed of heptasyllabic lines. Brevity is the soul of a Chinese poem, which is valued not so much for what it says as for what it suggests.

Li Ch'ing-chao begins the poem by asking why she is so homesick at the end of spring. She does not answer directly, but "the end of spring" suggests the reason. It calls forth such images as the fleeting of youth and the decline of days of beauty, and stirs up remembrances and nostalgia, "mixing memory and desire," as T. S. Eliot says in "The Waste Land."

In the second line, the poetess declares that she is ill, too weak to comb her hair. Her feebleness and listlessness form a sharp contrast with the babbling and thoughtlessness of the high-spirited swallows. With this in the foreground, the fourth line "When the gentle wind sweeps by, rose-scented is my screen," forms a beautiful background.

Modeled on *Sheng Ch'a Tzu**

Year after year in front of my jade mirror,
Wearily, I adorn my court-styled coiffure with plum flowers.

* As the meaning of the title is unclear to me, it has been left untranslated.

As he is not returning this year,
I dare not peruse his letters from south of the river.

Ever since his absence, I rarely touch wine.
On account of chagrin, my tears go dry.
Imagining the heavy clouds of the Kingdom of Ch'u,
Methinks he is farther away than the limit of the sky.

The first three words of the first line, "year after year," suggest
the long and frequent absences of her husband. The second line
vividly depicts the state of mind of the forlorn spouse who, during the absence of her husband, is not in the mood to concern
herself with make-up. The third and fourth lines state that the
poetess is afraid of receiving her husband's letters from the southern bank of the Yangtze River, lest they should increase her sadness.

The first two lines of the second stanza form an antithetical
couplet, which shows us that the bereaved wife is inconsolable.
She is no longer interested in wine and has wept so much that
there are no tears left.

The Kingdom of Ch'u was an ancient geographic name denoting South China. At the time of this poem, Chao Ming-ch'eng
was south while his wife was left in the north.

The last line is the climax, a most original expression. Staring
at the horizon and thinking of the heavy clouds hiding the Kingdom of Ch'u from sight, she thinks that her husband is even
farther away than the horizon, since the former is hidden from
sight while the latter is within easy reach of her eyes.

Li Ch'ing-chao finally joined her husband in Nanking, but
exile increased the longing for her home town. Feeling old and
weary, she turned down the invitations of friends, and thought
nostalgically of the days gone by when she and her girlhood
friends in rich array rivaled the flowers in elegance and coquetry.

In 1128, the second year of the reign of Emperor Kao-tsung,
Chao Ming-ch'eng, who had resigned during a period of mourn-
ing, reassumed office in Nanking as magistrate. The next year,
having been appointed magistrate of Huchow in Chekiang Province, he made plans to move his family to the valley of the Kan
River in Kiangsi. In March, they set out by ship first for Wuhu
in the province of Anhuei and then for Kushu in the same province. In May, they arrived in Ch'ih-yang; there Chao Ming-ch'eng

left the ship in order to proceed alone to his new post in Huchow. As he reached land, his wife waved farewell to him from the boat. Disturbed by a presentiment of misfortune, she asked him: "What shall I do if the city Ch'ih-yang is threatened by the enemy?"

From the river bank, he answered: "Follow the others. If you are obliged to give up part of our possessions, leave first the heavy things, then the clothes and bedclothes, then the books, then the scrolls, and then the antiques. But take with you the sacrificial vases. They should live or die with us. Do not forget!"

Then he hurried away on horseback. After a month's journey, he arrived in Nanking suffering from malaria and dysentery, which was caused by fatigue and hot weather. Receiving the news of his illness at the end of July, Li Ch'ing-chao joined him in Nanking. He never recovered, and died on the eighteenth of August at the age of forty-eight. Before passing away, he asked for a brush with which to write a poem, but left no testament.

IV   *The Widowhood of Li Ch'ing-chao*

Li Ch'ing-chao was now left alone amidst disorder and hostility. It was autumn. The sorrows of the bereaved widow found an echo in the melancholy of the season.

Modeled on *Andante*

Searching, searching,
Seeking, seeking,
Alone, alone,
Solitary, solitary,
Sad, sad,
Grieved, grieved,
Mournful, mournful.
The season is now warm, now cool,
The most difficult to bear.
Two or three cups of light wine
Resist not the rapid evening wind.
The wild geese pass by
And grieve my heart,
For they are old acquaintances.

The soil is loaded with yellow chrysanthemums.
Withered and spoiled,

> Who cares to pluck them?
> Alone I wait by the window.
> How can the day get dark?
> At dusk, the fine rain on the plane tree
> Falls drop by drop, drop by drop.
> To express all this,
> Can the mere word "sadness" suffice?

This poem can be considered a masterpiece from every point of view. Simple in appearance, sober in language, it is rich and profound in sensibility. All the symbols of autumn are assembled therein: the capricious weather, the rapid evening wind, the pattering rain, the wild geese piping forth a mournful sound. Since the death of her husband, the poetess is no longer interested in the flowers she once liked so much. The abandoned chrysanthemums have the same symbolic value as the dust-covered mirror or the neglected coiffure of the solitary widow.

This poem is also an original invention from the musical point of view. At the very beginning, the poetess uses fourteen repeated words to emphasize the mournful atmosphere. This repetition finds an echo towards the end of the poem in another repetition, "drop by drop, drop by drop." It is deplorable that in every language there is always something untranslatable, usually the essential. For instance, in Chinese the repetition "drop by drop, drop by drop" imitates perfectly the intermittent dripping of the rain, because of the fact that Chinese is monosyllabic. Phonetically translated, the words "drop by drop, drop by drop" sound like this: *tien tien ti ti*. Unfortunately, even phonetically translated, the charm of this imitation of sound cannot be rendered perfectly in English or in any other language, since the foreign reader will pronounce the romanized Chinese words in his own way.

There is another point that deserves passing notice. In this *tz'u*, most of the repeated words and the rhymed words belong to the group of sharps, and by their sharpness show the intensity and violence of pain. Finally, the first fourteen repeated words have a very pleasant rhythm, thanks to the intermingling of sharps and flats.

After her husband's burial, Li Ch'ing-chao did not know where to go. The beauties of the court harem had already scattered, and it was rumored that the Yangtze River would be blockaded. Li Ch'ing-chao was then seriously ill, on the brink of death. She

still owned twenty thousand books and two thousand volumes
of reproductions of stele inscriptions. She had most of the books
sent to Chao Ming-ch'eng's brother-in-law, who commanded the
garrison in Nan-ch'ang, Kiangsi Province. When the Chin took
Nan-ch'ang in December, all the books were lost. Only a small
number of light books and scrolls, several volumes containing
reproductions of stone inscription, and a dozen sacrificial vases,
which she had kept in her bedroom, were preserved from de-
struction.

As she could not risk sailing north, and since the Chin were
unpredictable, Li Ch'ing-chao tried to join her brother Li Hang
in Chekiang Province. When she arrived in Linghai, the magistrate had already abandoned the city to the enemy. Leaving her
belongings, she fled to Yung-chai, Shao-hsing, and Ch'ü-hsien, all
in the same province. In March 1131, she went back to Shao-
hsing, and in 1132 she went again to Hangchow. Finally she
settled down with her brother in Chin-hua. There she wrote one
of her best poems, reflecting the sadness and solitude of her old
age.

Modeled on *Spring in Wuling*

The wind is calm, the soil is perfumed, the flowers are fallen.
The day is dying, I am too weary to comb my hair.
Things remain, he is no longer here, all is finished.
Fain would I speak,
But tears precede my words.

They say spring still is in Double Stream.
Fain would I sail a boat there.
Only I fear that the small boat of the Double Stream
Could not bear so much sadness.

Li Ch'ing-chao is a great lover of nature. She is not only sensitive to beautiful scenery but also to the sweet odor of the flowers.
That is why she can smell the perfume of the earth covered with
fallen petals.

In the second line, there is again the weariness that has become
an obssession with her. All is finished. She cannot even speak without being choked by the flow of tears. Nevertheless, she still has
a strong desire to enjoy the spring, which is in full sway in Double Stream, despite her weariness. But she is very sad; and the

expression of her sadness is ingenious. She does not speak directly or effusively of her sorrow, but rather suggests it by evoking the image of a small boat sinking under the heavy load of woe.

Good fortune does not arrive in pairs, calamities walk hand in hand, says a Chinese proverb. Lonely and homeless, the aged poetess, involved in an incident concerning a jade pot, narrowly escaped imprisonment.

It is to be recalled that when Chao Ming-ch'eng was ill, a member of the Imperial Academy named Chang Fei-ch'ing came to inquire after his health. Chang took along with him a false jade pot. When he left Chao's house, he was seen carrying the jade pot, pretending to have discovered it within the premises. The patient was calumniously accused of bribing the Chin with the pot in order to conspire against the Southern Sung dynasty. After the death of Chao Ming-ch'eng, Li Ch'ing-chao was seized with fear and wanted to submit all of her possessions to the court to be examined. She no longer dared to keep the antiques and manuscripts with her and had them sent to Ch'en-hsien. When the imperial army defeated the enemy there, these objects were said to have been seized by a certain General Li. As a result, nothing survived the plunder except seven cases of books, paintings, and ink slabs. These books were dear to her because of the annotations of Chao Ming-ch'eng, and Li Ch'ing-chao always put them under her bed. Unfortunately, one night a burglar made an opening in the wall and purloined five of the seven cases. The chagrined poetess offered a large reward to get them back. Two days later, a neighbor called Chung Fu-hao came to her with eighteen scrolls and asked for money in recompense. She knew then that the thief was not far away, but she never recovered the rest of the stolen goods.

It is highly deplorable that references to Li Ch'ing-chao's life should be so sparse. We are not much enlightened by the history of the Sung, which devoted only a limited space to China's feminine genius. Ancient critics spoke only briefly of her, and modern critics cannot be more explicit because of lack of documentation. Little can be traced; even the date of her death remains unknown to posterity. We know nothing about her from her fifty-third year onward, and the rumor about her remarriage with Chang Ju-chou has never been proved. She probably died in distress and misery, but her spirit did not perish, for it remains in the beauty of her poetry.

CHAPTER 3

The Works of Li Ch'ing-chao

I *Li Ch'ing-chao as a Lyric Poet*

A GREAT poet should have three fundamental qualities: sensibility, ideals, and creative power. Without sensibility, a poet would not be able to endow his works with life. Without lofty ideals, a poet would not be able to endow his works with a transcendental character. Without creative power, a poet would not be a real poet but only an imitator of his forerunners or contemporaries. Under the Sung, when few poets possessed these qualities, Li Ch'ing-chao was one who did. It is universally accepted that Li Ch'ing-chao is China's greatest poetess. Her delicate sensibility, her keen observation, her profound love of nature, her clear and simple language, her original imagery and expression, and, above all, her rich experience in life made her worthy of this title.

In order to appreciate her works, we must first understand her as a woman. A many-sided genius, she was not only a great *tz'u* composer but also an excellent prose writer, musician, and painter. Ch'en tzu-liang of the Ming dynasty had a painting by her illustrating the Tang poet Po Chu-i's famous poem entitled *The Song of the Guitar,* and Mo Yen-han owned one of her paintings of bamboo. Nevertheless, her genius and erudition did not deprive her of femininity. She remained a woman: she was elegant and coquettish; she sang bewitchingly; she played various musical instruments. In short, she was an accomplished lady.

In ancient China, where most women lived in seclusion and were by tradition kept in ignorance, Li Ch'ing-chao had the good fortune to live as a free human being. She came from a bourgeois family and was given an education just as though she were a boy. She had a happy childhood. Her marriage was a successful one; she loved her husband dearly and lived with him in perfect harmony and equality. Her experiences in life were abundant. She knew the tenderness of love, the sadness of separation; experienced the miseries of war; traveled far and wide; and was condemned to loneliness and wandering in her old age. She felt deeply and lived intensely, and emotion occupies, therefore, an important place in her *tz'u*. She delivered no message, developed no theory, and was not interested in moralizing. Her works contain neither philosophical abstractions nor social-minded concepts. She was by nature romantic and artistic. In spite of her erudition, she was neither a scholar nor a philosopher. She was simply a poet, purely lyric and esthetic. Every line of her poetry revealed the quivering of a delicate feminine soul.

The three dominant traits of Li Ch'ing-chao's character were a deep love of nature, a profound sensibility, and a strong desire to be free and natural. In ancient Sung China, where women with bound feet were confined to the inner rooms, Li Ch'ing-chao lived in complete freedom. She loved the green earth with its infinite beauty; she listened to the melodious chirping of birds among the trees; she watched with delight the sinking sun, the gathering clouds, and the intricate process of the blooming of flowers in her garden. As her home city was one of lakes, willows, and lotus, she sailed alone or in the company of others to enjoy the natural scenery. She liked sports. She used to play on the swings until her silk robe was soaked with perspiration. When she was in Nanking, on snowy days, clad in a palm-leaf cloak and wearing a bamboo-plaited hat, she sometimes walked as far as the suburbs in search of inspiration. Because of this profound love of nature, she wrote exquisite verse about mountains and lakes, birds and flowers, and the ever-changing scene of the passing seasons and natural phenomena. The following poem about red plum flowers shows the extent to which Li Ch'ing-chao was a friend of the flowers:

Modeled on *The Fisherman's Pride*

In the snow, I already know spring's message,
The jade boughs of the plum tree being adorned
        with delicate blossoms.
Half-open, their scented face is full of charm.
In the middle of the garden,
They look like beauties just coming out of a bath.

On purpose, the Creator made the moon shine
Bright as a precious stone.
Newly-brewed wine in goblets of gold;
Let's drink and fear not tipsiness,
For tonight we celebrate an incomparable flower.

We can see from the poem above the detail in which Li Ch'ing-chao paints her favorite flower. She knows that spring is not far away since the plum tree, herald of the wondrous season, is in bloom. In order to show the elegance of the plum tree and its blossoms, she likens the boughs to jade, while the half-open blossoms are compared to the beautiful face of a woman whose skin is perfumed, delicate, and smooth. Moreover, the flowers are so fresh that they look like beauties just coming out of a bath. As moonlight enhances the beauty of the plum flowers, Li Ch'ing-chao expresses her gratitude to the Creator for the shaft of light, which she compares to the glistening of a precious stone. She then invites her husband to drink with her to their hearts' content because she wants to celebrate the blooming of this incomparable flower, symbol of nobility.

This poem about plum flowers, purely esthetic and sensual, is representative of Chinese descriptive poetry. The Chinese poet limits his description to outward beauty without going into the depth of what he describes. In this connection, I should like to quote two stanzas by Emily Dickinson on flowers:

> To pack the bud, oppose the worm,
> Obtain its right of dew,
> Adjust the heat, elude the wind,
> Escape the prowling bee,
>
> Great nature not to disappoint,
> Awaiting her that day—
> To be a flower is profound
> Responsibility!

From the comparative study of these two poems, we can state that Chinese poetry is characterized by concreteness and that it excludes the domain of abstraction. The Chinese poet describes what is visible rather than what is invisible.

In former days, the only feminine wine drinkers were the courtesans who accompanied men of letters. However, wine seemed to be a favorite drink of our poetess as well, for she used beautiful words in praise of it:

Newly-brewed wine in goblets of gold.

Let not the deep cup be filled with amber-colored wine!

In tipsiness, I adorn myself with plum flowers.

Awakening from tipsiness, I prefer bitter tea.

My home town I forget not, save in tipsiness.

Two or three cups of wine resist not the rapid evening wind.

Wine is worried when sorrows are heavy.

As readers of Chinese poetry may note, the word *chiu* (wine)
and the word *tsui* are often associated with the poems of such
great wine lovers as Li Po and T'ao Ch'ien. The word *tsui* is usually translated as "drunk," but it has a slightly different meaning;
it does not imply gross sensual enjoyment nor does it suggest hi-
larity or riotousness. It refers only to the escape through wine
from the miseries of the world into oblivion, and from one's personal emotions and normal anxieties. Therefore, wherever there
are references to drinking and to becoming *tsui* in Li Ch'ing-
chao's poetry, I have translated the word *tsui* as "tipsiness" or as
"being tipsy," to distinguish it from the word "drunk," which usually carries an unpleasant implication or association.

Li Ch'ing-chao drank on happy occasions:

Modeled on *As In a Dream*

Often, in the river bank pavilion, at dusk,
Drowsy with wine, we know not our way home.
At the height of bliss, homeward we sail
But our nocturnal boat penetrates by error into
    the depth of lotus flowers.
Pushing ahead, pushing ahead,
We wake up the sea gulls and herons of the bank.

This poem shows that Li Ch'ing-chao loves outdoor life. She
likes to sail and to roam about scenic places. Her experience in
life forms the woof and warp of her poetry, and she does not rely
upon fancy in her poems. For these reasons, her works are devoid
of artificiality.

She also counts on wine to drown her sorrows:

Modeled on *Partridges in the Sky*

The cool sun climbs up my window adorned with swastikas.
The plane tree should loathe last night's frost.
After tipsiness, I prefer bitter tea;
Awakening from my dream, I find incense desirable.
Autumn is gone, still lengthy is the day.
Like Wang Ts'an I am homesick.
'Tis better to get tipsy as usual
And enjoy the yellow chrysanthemums near the east hedge.

In ancient China, window frames and balustrades were usually adorned with swastikas. It is late autumn. The plane tree in Li Ch'ing-chao's garden is covered with frost. Even the sunbeams climbing up the window seem cool. Autumn, season of frost, desolation, and blight! All the rich luxuriance of green is changed, all the flowers swept down to earth. Autumn is the season that arouses cares and sorrows, stirs memories, and causes homesickness. Kept from slumber by the melancholy of autumn, our poetess prefers drinking away her sorrow in the company of chrysanthemums, the only flower that blooms in defiance of frost and storm.

In China, chrysanthemums are highly esteemed by men of letters because they are symbols of pride, solitude, and fortitude. In autumn, when the flowers are faded and gone, chrysanthemums alone bloom in spite of cold weather. Consequently, they are considered to have the qualities required of men of letters and particularly of poets: solitude, nobility of soul, and distinction. For this reason, Li Ch'ing-chao admired this noble flower and wrote prolifically about it.

In another poem, she complains that a sound sleep did not dissipate the effect of wine:

Modeled on *As In a Dream*

Last night, the rain was light, the wind sudden.
A heavy slumber did not dissipate my tipsiness.
I ask the one who rolls up the screen how the begonias are.
She says they are as of yore.
"Know you not? Know you not?
"Tis time when green should be fat and the red thin."

This *tz'u* is comprised of only thirty-three words. Despite its conciseness, it attains perfection from every point of view. Metrically speaking, the poem is harmonious and strictly conforms to rules governing the arrangement of tones. And the poem itself is such a vivid picture that it produces a dramatic effect. The first line denotes time: a late spring with fine rain and sudden wind. During the night, after drinking, our poetess fell into a profound sleep. Awakening in the morning, she still remembers last night's wind and rain, which must have spoiled the begonias. Being a great lover of flowers, she is worried about the begonias and asks her maidservant about them. The maid, quite indifferent to their fate, answers absent-mindedly that they are just the same. Then the poetess becomes impatient and emphatically replies, "Don't you know that the wind must have ruined the flowers, while the rain fattened the leaves?" But instead of using the words "leaves" and "flowers," she uses the adjectives "green" and "red," just as she employs the word "thin" to denote the withered flowers, and the word "fat" to denote the glistening leaves washed by the rain.

As has already been mentioned, there existed between the poetess and her husband real love and perfect harmony. This constituted a rare exception in conjugal life in ancient China, where spiritual communion between husband and wife was nearly impossible. The reason was that the men, at least those of high station, were usually cultured, while the women were generally ignorant.

But Li Ch'ing-chao's marriage was different. There existed between the spouses not only a deep affection but also a continuous intellectual relationship. She was not only on an equal plane with her husband, but she even outshone him in the composition of verse. While Chao Ming-ch'eng was absent, Li Ch'ing-chao once sent him a letter containing this poem:

Modeled on *Tipsy Among the Flowers*

(The Double Ninth Festival)

Thin fog, heavy clouds, sad and endless is the day.
Here again is the Double Ninth Festival.
Last night, coolness first penetrated the precious
pillow and the muslin bed curtains.

> Having drunk wine near the east hedge at dusk,
> My sleeves are imbued with a discreet perfume.
> Say not it is not heart-rending.
> When the west wind stirs the screen,
> I am as frail as the yellow chrysanthemums.

In China, the ninth moon is the season of chrysanthemums. On the ninth day of the ninth moon by the lunar calendar, poets drink wine near the east hedge, where chrysanthemums are supposed to be planted. In spite of the absence of Chao Ming-ch'eng, Li Ch'ing-chao still observes the poets' tradition of drinking in front of the chrysanthemums.

In the first line, thin fog and heavy clouds create a melancholy atmosphere. The day seems sad and endless to Li Ch'ing-chao in the absence of her husband. In the second line, the words "here again" suggest that time is fleeting, even though the day seems interminable. In the third line, we note that the weather has changed. Coolness has set in with the Double Ninth Festival, and our poetess feels cold in body and soul. The last two lines are the best. Though simple in appearance, they reach an unusually elevated realm of pathetic beauty.

Chao Ming-ch'eng admired this *tz'u* so much that he shut himself up for three days and refused either to receive guests or to attend to official business in order to compose some fifteen poems with a view to competing with his wife. He then mixed his own poems with the one she had sent him and showed them to his friend Lu Te-fu in order to ask his opinion. After having read them carefully, Chao's friend declared that there were only two good lines. When he eagerly asked him what they were, his friend replied: "When the west wind stirs the screen,/I am as frail as the yellow chrysanthemums."

Fortunately, Chao Ming-ch'eng was not an egoist, and the knowledge of his being a minor poet did not mar the harmony between the spouses. When they were together, Li Ch'ing-chao wrote delicate and tender verses in praise of love:

Modeled on *Plucking the Mulberries*

In the evening, a puff of wind mingled with rain
Washed away the heat of the day.

Having stopped playing on the *sheng* and *huang*,*
Slightly, slightly, I paint my cheeks in front of the mirror.

Through the thin red silk appears my skin,
White as jade, pure as snow, smooth and perfumed.
Smiling, I say to my beloved:
Tonight, the muslin bed curtains, the mat and the pillows
    will be cool.

Li Ch'ing-chao wrote this poem shortly after her marriage. It
was one of the happiest moments in her life. She was in the flower
of youth. The roses of her cheeks blushed bright, and her rounded
arms were dazzling white. She was newly wed, tender, and affectionate. Can anything reveal better a young bride's tender heart
than the line, "Tonight, the muslin bed curtains, the mat and
pillows will be cool"?

The whole poem centers in summer. The air has been sticky
and stifling. Quite unexpectedly, a puff of wind mingled with rain
washes away the day's heat and heralds a cool night. After she
has finished playing the musical instrument, she busies herself
with make-up in front of her mirror, which reflects her rosy
cheeks, cherry lips, and white skin. The poem comes to a climax
when, coquettishly smiling, she whispers to her husband that the
pillows and mat will be cool when night sets in, suggesting that
it will be an ideal night for lovers.

But happiness never lasts. Shortly after her marriage, Chao
Ming-ch'eng, who was still a young student, had to absent himself frequently from home. His bride pined for him within the inner chamber. Deeply grieved by his absence, Li Ch'ing-chao
wrote touching verses:

Modeled on *Nostalgia of the Flute in the Phoenix Pavilion*

Incense is chilled in the lion-shaped gold burner.
My coverlet unfurls its red waves.
Though up from my couch, I am too weary to comb my hair.
Let the dust cover my precious coiffure,
And the sun climb up the hooks of my bed curtains.

* *Sheng and huang:* These two words, though often mentioned together,
denote a single instrument, the *sheng, huang* being the copper leaves (or the
reed) fixed inside the instrument. The *sheng* is an ancient Chinese musical
instrument made of bamboo pipes arranged in such a way that it looks like
the fingers on a hand.

I most fear the bitter sorrow of separation.
So much to tell, yet I keep silent.
I have become more slender of late,
Neither on account of being ill with drinking,
Nor due to the melancholy of autumn.

Finished, finished!
This time he is gone.
Farewell songs repeated a thousand times did not keep him
    from parting.
My thoughts are with him in Wuling,
My pavilion of Ch'in is sealed by fog.
Only the flowing water in front of the pavilion
Knows that my eyes are fixed thereupon all day long.
Where there are my strained eyes,
There is a newborn chagrin.

This *tz'u* also belongs to the cycle of separation. Alone, she lies
in her inner chamber. Awakened from slumber, up from her
couch, she feels the same weariness: she does not wipe the
dust covering her dressing table; she dallies in bed and gets up
late when the sun is already high. She avoids speaking of her husband so as not to increase the sorrow of separation. She finds that
she has lost weight, neither because of being ill from drinking,
nor because of the melancholy season of autumn, but because of
her husband's absence. He is far away in Wuling—an ancient geographic name denoting South China. (The geographic names
"Wuling" and "Ch'in" are only symbolic; they do not really mean
that Chao Ming-ch'eng is in Wuling while Li Ch'ing-chao is in
Shensi, but only suggest that the lovers are separated by a long
distance.) She is in her pavilion in the north. What can she do but
strive to pierce with strained eyes the distance between them?

The poems devoted to the theme of separation are moving and
pathetic, but they are illumined with hope. But those written in
her widowhood represent the mournful cries of an agonized soul:

Modeled on *Strolling in the Royal Street*

In the morning I get up from my wicker bed covered
    with paper curtains.
To tell my chagrin, words suffice not,
Good ideas are wanting.

The scent of sandalwood is gone, the jade burner chilled
To harmonize with my heart cold as water,
Three notes break from a lute,
Waking up the plum flowers.
What a springtime atmosphere!

The whispering breeze, the pattering rain
Force a thousand lines of tears from my eyes.
The flutist is gone, the jade pavilion empty.
I pluck a branch of flowers,
No one to send them to,
Neither on earth nor in heaven.

This is really a widow's poem, for "wicker" bed and "paper" curtains form a sharp contrast with the "precious" pillows and "jade" mat she used to mention. Of course, such words as "wicker" and "paper" should not be taken literally as meaning that her bed is made of wicker and that her bed curtains are made of paper. In Chinese poetry, adjectives have symbolic value. In her happy days, she used the word "emerald" to qualify screen and the word "orchid" to modify boat. Candles and halls were "painted," goblets were "of gold," balustrades were "sculptured." These adjectives denoted not only elegance and sumptuousness but also blissfulness and gaiety. In her widowhood, she would no longer speak of phoenix hairpins nor talk about silk robes.

"The flutist is gone, the jade pavilion empty" is a line that needs explanation. Chinese poets are rarely outspoken, which is why they resort to allusion. Allusion refers to historical personages and events, legends and myths, and can be employed as an economical means of presenting a situation. Here the "flutist" refers to the son-in-law of Duke Mu of the Kingdom of Ch'in of the feudal period. He was a skilful flutist and imitated perfectly on his instrument the singing of the phoenix, the traditional sacred bird. His father-in-law therefore had a pavilion built for him called the Phoenix Pavilion. One day, while he was playing the flute in the company of his wife, he attracted a phoenix who carried them both away on its wing. In this poem, the flutist is Chao Ming-ch'eng, and the allusion is used to provide contrast. The flutist left with his wife, but Chao Ming-ch'eng left alone without taking with him the bereaved spouse.

For the poets, from Dante to Villon to T. S. Eliot, Time has always been an obsession. They are always haunted by the idea of the division of Time; past, present, and future. The Romantic poets regret the passing of blossoming youth and deplore the coming of doddering age. Modern writers such as Eliot, Proust, and Kierkegaard dream of an eternal instant, the fulness of which abolishes duration. But Chinese poets are not metaphysicians; they do not lose themselves in a labyrinth of abstraction. This too is true of Li Ch'ing-chao. She deplored the fading of spring, grieved over the coming of autumn, and was sensitive to the falling of spring petals, the withering of autumn leaves, the glimmering of the setting sun, and the rolling of Time's winged chariot:

Modeled on *Fairies on the River Bank*

Profound, profound is my courtyard, how profound?
Wrapped in clouds and fog, my windows and doors are shut.
Little by little new willows and plum blossoms appear.
Spring is back on the boughs in Mo-ling,
Old age is coming to me in the city of Chien-k'ang.

How I used to sing of moon and breeze!
Today I chant naught, aged and gray.
Who pities a withered creature?
Neither is my heart set on trying the lamp
Nor on treading snow.

As has already been mentioned, Li Ch'ing-chao formerly liked to be out-of-doors; now voluntary seclusion marks the turning point in her life. She was then in Nanking, "Chien-k'ang" and "Mo-ling" being its ancient names. It is springtime. The willows have tender leaves, the plum trees are in bloom. Spring is back once more, but her youth is gone forever. She thinks of bygone days when, young and lighthearted, she wrote many poems in praise of moon and breeze. Today, old and weary, she is indifferent to all because joy is lost at the thought that youth has slipped away and that old age is coming.

Readers of Chinese poetry must have noticed the abundance of poems on nostalgia. Chinese poets seem to be perpetually lamenting their exile and manifesting the desire to return home. This longing is not mere sentimentality, if one bears in mind the vastness of Chinese territory, the difficulties of communication in ancient times, and the importance of the family in traditional Chinese society. Therefore, it is not surprising that homesickness should become a constant theme in Chinese poetry. Like most Chinese, Li Ch'ing-chao was deeply attached to her native home. When she joined her husband in the south, she thought nostalgically of North China where, as a young maid, she enjoyed the company of feminine companions:

Modeled on *The Eternal Joy of Meeting*

The melting gold of the sinking sun,
The gathering jade of the evening clouds.
Where is he?
Heavy fog soaking the willows,
Mournful notes of a flute playing the tune "Plum Flower,"
What a springtime atmosphere!
'Tis the Lantern Festival.
Mild is the weather.
Will there be no wind or rain at this moment?
My drinking companions and poet friends
Came with perfumed chariots and precious horses,
But I declined their invitation.

When the Empire was prosperous,
We ladies were much at leisure,
And highly valued the fifteenth day of each moon.
Wearing emerald-adorned coiffures
And gold-threaded, willowlike, snow-white belts,
We rivaled one another in elegance.
Today I am withered,
With windy hair and frost temples.
I dare not go among the flowers,
But prefer listening to others' speeches and laughter
Across my bamboo screen.

This poem begins with two brilliant images: the melting gold of the sinking sun; the gathering jade of the evening clouds. The precision of imagery, mastery of language, and keen observation merit profound admiration. This poem was probably written during Chao Ming-ch'eng's absence, since she asks, "Where is he?" It is springtime, but spring is disheartening for her; for she is far away from both her husband and her home. Her friends come to invite her out, but she finds no solace in their company;

she thinks of her home, where as a young girl she enjoyed going out dressed in rich array with her friends. Today, the Central Plain has been taken by the enemy. She is lonely and in exile; her hair is gray and disheveled. Everything conspires against her. How can she, who used to rival the flowers in beauty, go among them at this moment, when she is faded and dull?

II   *The Esthete*

Li Ch'ing-chao did not establish a theory of art nor express esthetic ideas, but everything about her person and her style was esthetic: she wrote as her feelings led her to do, and her poems spoke more eloquently than any abstract essays on esthetics. She was a many-sided artist and led a very artistic life in the company of her husband. She played the lute well and she could also sing; the lines of her poetry were fluent and harmonious as a consequence. Li Ch'ing-chao was also a good painter. She had keen observation, her images were well-molded, her descriptions minute and precise, and her poems had the value of the plastic arts. As she was also an excellent phonetician, she attached great importance to the auditory effect of language in poetry. Her models were well-chosen, her tone pattern and rhyme scheme carefully studied. She took no liberty with regard to the arrangement of tones or subtones. Each of her poems, therefore, is a piece of magnificent architecture, solid and unshakable.

Let us now examine some of her poems esthetically:

A New Version of *Washing Brook Sand*
(*The Kuei Flower*)

Thousands of light specks of gold,
A myriad of well-cut leaves of jade.
You have the air of Yen Fu,
How bright!

Plum blossoms seem too vulgar,
Lilacs seem too melancholy.
But your strong perfume keeps me from dreaming afar;
How cruel!

This *tz'u* is written in praise of the *kuei* flower, which probably belongs to the family of laurels. The flowers, tiny and yellow, look like specks of gold. Li Ch'ing-chao, who has a strong predilection for this flower, likens it to Yen Fu, a person of dazzling intelligence who lived during the Six Dynasty period. And the comparison is perfect. She says that the plum flowers seem vulgar and that the lilacs seem melancholy in the presence of the *kuei*, but she denounces it for its strong perfume, which keeps her awake and prevents her from dreaming of her husband, who is a thousand miles away. In this *tz'u*, the accuracy and originality of comparison, and the contrast between the *kuei* flower and the plum blossoms and lilacs deserve our admiration.

The following *tz'u* was written immediately after her marriage. She is young, with a face as fair as a flower and movements full of grace. It is a spring night. The young bride, in nocturnal array, is boating on a river covered with peach blossoms. As she is a good singer, she sings coquettishly so as to captivate her lover's heart. But the spring night is too short. Soon they have to sail homeward, and the bride gazes regretfully at the moon, which casts its rays over their boat:

Modeled on *Waves Wash Away the Sand*

Wont am I to bind my slender waist,
Too frail to bear the melancholy of spring.
The plum flowers cast their shadows on my person in
   nocturnal array.
Graceful, slim, what can I be likened to?
A trail of blue clouds.

While sailing on the river covered with peach blossoms,
Opening my vermilion lips, how skilfully I sing!
Every word is coquetry and charm.
My eyes turned to the sky, regretfully I gaze at the moon
Shining upon our boat of return.

From the foregoing poem, we can see how esthetically she lived, how carefully she adorned herself. When we read this poem, we can imagine a perfect picture, with the poetess herself in the foreground. The surroundings are fairylike. The spring night is in all its splendor. The moon sheds its silver rays on the river where the barge glides under an arbor of peach blossoms. The poetess, elegant, coquettish, richly arrayed, and freshly made up, opens her cherrylike lips to sing a beautiful song.

Yes, she really lived those happy moments and wove them into her poems. Consequently, the esthetic experience of Li Ch'ing-chao lies in the expression of the emotions felt and in the enjoyment of the emotions expressed in her poems. If we choose to speak in terms of modern philosophy, let us say that she has immortalized those happy moments, realized the infinite in the finite.

Another poem, simple and plain in appearance, is rich in sensibility and musicality.

Modeled on *Plucking the Mulberries*

I planted banana trees in front of my window.
Their shade fills up the courtyard.
Their shade fills up the courtyard.
Leaves, leaves! Hearts, hearts!
Now rolled, now unrolled, the leaves evoke the emotions
    of human hearts.

Grieving is the midnight rain upon my pillow.
Every drop is sadness.
Every drop is sadness.
Worn by absence,
I am loath to get up to listen.

In this *tz'u*, Li Ch'ing-chao employs a great number of repeated words and sentences. The repeated lines, "Their shade fills up the courtyard, their shade fills up the courtyard," are not only pleasing to the ear but also suggest the luxuriance of the foliage. The repeated words, "Leaves, leaves! Hearts, hearts!" pronounced as if in a sigh, sound beautiful and pathetic. Then the poetess likens the banana leaves to human hearts. We human beings with our joy and pain are now lighthearted, now heavyhearted, just as the banana leaves are now rolled, now unrolled. Finally, the repeated lines, "Every drop is sadness, every drop is sadness," are an imitation of the dripping rain.

In another *tz'u*, Li Ch'ing-chao uses ordinary words from beginning to end. But under her touch, as if by magic, the commonplace is transmuted into wonder. Although simple in appearance, this poem is most touching:

Modeled on *As In a Dream*

Who sits by the lit window?
Two of us: my shadow and I.

At bedtime, the lamp wick being burned out,
Even my shadow forsakes me.
What to do? What to do?
Poor me!

As mentioned before, everything about Li Ch'ing-chao was esthetic. She found pleasure in adorning her hair with plum flowers; she was fond of beautiful clothes; she painted; she enjoyed
singing and playing musical instruments; she took delight in con-
templating the flowers and birds and in loitering about the
countryside. Above all, she enjoyed weaving the color and music of her soul into her works, so that her poems are possessed of
musical harmony, pictorial beauty, and architectural structure.

III *Themes*

Li Ch'ing-chao was a pure lyric poet, with limited inspiration.
The themes of her poetic works were built upon love: love for
her husband, love for nature, love for her native home. Her love
for her mate is expressed in the following:

Modeled on *Grudge Against the Lord*

My dream is gone, the clepsydra is stilled.
Coolness is born on my pillow,
The emerald screen faces the dawn.
Who has swept the fallen petals out-of-doors?
Last night's wind.

The sound of the jade flute is stilled; where is he?
Spring is gone again,
How could he bear to stay away from home?
This love of mine, this grudge of mine,
Fain would I confide to the passing clouds
And the God of Spring.

Waking at daybreak, the poetess lies in solitude within her inner chamber. She has drunk wine before going to bed. When she
awakens, the effect of the wine is gone, and her heavy sorrows are
not submerged. There is continuous longing for her husband, but
she does not tell us so directly in the first stanza; but what is
merely implied is just as impressive: "Coolness is born on my pillow." She feels cold, perhaps less physically than spiritually. In

the second stanza, however, she is impatient and becomes out-spoken. She asks where he is, why he puts off his date of return. She even wants to tell the passing clouds about her feelings and to ask the God of Spring why her husband lingers abroad. Her love for Chao Ming-ch'eng is profound; profound too is the re-sentment she bears against him because of his frequent and pro-longed absence. This weight of love and grudge requires expres-sion; that expression is art.

Nature is an inexhaustible source of joy. It not only contains woods, lakes, and hills, but also those woods, lakes, and hills take a new form by contact with the poetess, who wraps them in a cloak of human emotion and unites with them. This world which takes its form from the mold of the poetess' perception becomes a world of her senses, emotions, and mind; partial but independ-ent, eternal and absolute:

Modeled on *Grudge Against the Lord*

The wind rises, the lake ripples far and wide.
Late autumn.
Flowers are few, fragrance is scanty.
The glow of water and the color of mountains become
    enamored of us.
To tell about their infinite charms,
Words suffice not.

Lotus seeds have ripened,
Lotus leaves are faded.
Flowers and weeds of the bank
Are soaked with dewdrops.
Sea gulls and herons of the bank turn their backs to us,
As if grudging our homeward faring.

In the following poem, it is early spring, the beginning of the wondrous season, and the poetess feels lighthearted because of the coming of the days of splendor. Nevertheless, high-spirited as she is, there is still the perpetual longing for home.

Modeled on *Buddhist Coiffure*

Gentle breeze, mild sun, early spring.
Lightly clad, lighthearted I suddenly feel.
Up from my couch, I am slightly shivery.
The plum flowers have died in my hair.

Whither is my native land?
I forget it not, save in tipsiness.
The sandalwood was burning during my slumber.
The scent is gone but the wine remains.

IV *The Language of the Poetess*

As has already been seen, Li Ch'ing-chao's poetry chiefly deals
with the flight of time, the sadness of parting, the love for her
husband, natural beauty, nostalgia, and solace in drinking. In poetry of such limited subject matter, language occupies a very important place, enabling the reader to forget the monotony of inspiration. And Li Ch'ing-chao is a master of her language.
Sometimes she simply looks around and describes what she
sees in very plain words, which under her magic touch become
infinitely poetic:

> Clouds flying to and fro, moonlight is dimned.
> At dusk, fine rain soaks the swing.

> The moon casts its rays athwart
> And soaks the pear flowers.

> A pool surrounded by verdant grass,
> A courtyard covered with green shades,
> The coolness of a fine evening penetrating the
>   muslin-veiled casement.

Sometimes she creates original images and invents new expressions:

> A goblet of spring.

> Double doors loaded with the shadows of flowers,
> Grossly plaited screen spread with pale moon,
> What a beauteous evening!

> A thousand skeins of sorrow bind my tender heart.

> The melting gold of the sinking sun,
> The gathering jade of the evening clouds.

Sometimes she relies upon the repetition of words to produce
musical and rhetorical effect. In a *tz'u* modeled on *Andante,* she
begins with fourteen repetitive words:

Searching, searching,
Seeking, seeking,
Lonely, lonely,
Solitary, solitary,
Sad, sad,
Grieved, grieved,
Mournful, mournful.

The repeated words were employed so naturally that she has won the admiration of many critics. "The fourteen repeated words sound like large and small pearls dropping onto a jade plate," said Hsü Hung-t'ing.

Li Ch'ing-chao's language is usually characterized by delicacy and elegance, but sometimes she also writes in a powerful style and leads us to a new world, a wider field of vision, a higher sphere of thought:

Modeled on *The Fisherman's Pride*

The sky, the waves of clouds, the morning mist blended
    in one.
The Milky Way was shimmering, a thousand sails were
    dancing.
Methinks I was borne to the throne of God.
"Whither are you going?" a celestial voice asked me.
Sighing, I replied: "Long, long is the way, the day is
    dying."
In vain, I compose astonishing verses.
The roc-bird is soaring upon the wind for a ninety-
    thousand-mile journey.

Stop not, O wind!
Blow my boat to fairyland.

This piece of work is powerful and visionary. The poem gives an account of a dream of the poetess and is based upon fancy and imagination. The flow of verse is as rapid as a galloping horse. In this regard, the critic Lung Mu-hsün says that Li Ch'ing-chao's poetry combines esthetic restraint with romantic abandonment.

From the examples given above, one cannot fail to see that Li Ch'ing-chao not only had great sensibility but also was able to express this quality in poetic language. With her natural gift for words, as well as acquired verbal skill, she created original images or relied upon simple language to convey effectively her feelings of bliss, idleness, or depression. The scenes and emotions she explored are universal and as old as mankind itself, but she was able to find new words to create new worlds. A poet's task is not simply to say something for the first time but also to say in a different manner what has been said a thousand times before. As Li Ch'ing-chao was a poet of limited inspiration, the literary value of her poetry lies chiefly in her great capacity to explore the possibilities of language.

V   *The Thinking of Li Ch'ing-chao*

Chinese poetry is said to have been highly influenced by the three principal oriental philosophies: Confucian morality, Taoist mysticism, and Buddhist nihilism. To Confucius, who preached humanitarianism and social harmony, who taught rites and good manners, who encouraged moderation of feeling and expression, and who distinguished good from evil, Chinese poetry owes its realistic, utilitarian, reasonable, and moral character. To Lao-tzu, the founder of Taoism, who preached quietude and non-activity, who recommended a detached attitude towards worldly vanities, and who invited us to return to nature, Chinese poetry owes its cosmic and transcendental character. According to Buddhism, life is suffering: birth, old age, illness, and death. Worldly pleasures are transient and ephemeral. Sounds, colors, scents, and tastes are merely illusions. Desire is the root of evil. Therefore, Buddhism teaches the suppression of desire in order to reach nirvana, or the extinction of the flames of life.

To these three guiding principles is added the individualist view of poetry as self-expression. Consequently, one may conclude that there are three traditional Chinese views on poetry: the didactic view attributed to Confucius, the philosophical view attributed to Taoist mysticism and Buddhist nihilism, and the individualist view, which advocates that poetry is nothing but the expression of the heart's desires, its emotions, and one's own personality.

For those who hold the didactic view, poetry is a kind of moral instruction and social comment. It should describe the suffering of the people, reflect their feeling toward the government, and expose social evil. For those with the philosophical view, poetry is the embodiment of the poet's contemplation of the world and of his own mind. A poet should always seek to attain that calm, contemplative state of mind. In other words, a poet should not assert his own personality but identify himself with the object of his contemplation, so that there is an overflowing of himself into the object of being contemplated. For those who hold the individualist view, poetry expresses one's nature and emotion. If its language moves the heart, if its color strikes the eye, if its flavor pleases the mouth, if its sound delights the ear, then it is good poetry. Thus, Chinese poetry is mainly social, philosophical, and lyrical. Its subject matter is very limited. It usually deals with emotion, natural beauty, warfare, the separation of friends or spouses, the flight of youth, the passing seasons, and altruistic or philosophical ideas.

Now let us examine the extent to which Li Ch'ing-chao was influenced by the above mentioned critical views on poetry. If Li Ch'ing-chao's poetry lacks that realistic, utilitarian, and moralizing character, which is usually attributed to Confucian morality, she observes, at least from the technical point of view, Confucius' teaching that poetry should be gentle, moderate, sincere, and deep. She expresses joy without licentiousness, grief without agony. And we may now study analytically, from this point of view, a short poem by Li Ch'ing-chao:

Modeled on *Painted Lips*

In the depth of my silent chamber,
A thousand skeins of sorrow bind my tender heart.
Spring I love but spring is gone,
Some raindrops sweep the flowers down to earth.

Leaning against the balustrade, shifting from one
    end to the other,
I am no less disheartened.
Whither is he?
Leaves of grass spread to the horizon
And hide from my eye the road of return.

This poem of Li Ch'ing-chao, so short and simple in appearance, is highly appreciated for its power of suggestion. In the first line, the word "depth" emphasizes the idea of solitude because the wider the space, the lonelier one feels. In the second line, sorrow is likened to entangled threads that bind the poetess' loving heart, and from which there is no escape. In the third line, spring is a symbol of youth. Our poetess loves youth, but youth does not linger on forever, just as flowers fall to earth at the end of spring. In the fourth line, the raindrop is a symbol of adversity. Flowers cannot elude raindrops, just as men cannot elude old age.

Overly oppressed by the silence that reigns in her inner chamber, the poetess then leaves it and leans against the balcony. She shifts from one place to another along the balustrade but does not feel more cheerful, nor does she find delight in the contemplation of nature, she who used to be a great lover of natural beauty. Why? Because it is the end of spring and Li Ch'ing-chao is saddened by the fleeting of the glorious days. Moreover, there is a continuous longing for her husband, and the sight of fallen flowers and raindrops reminds her of the passing of youth and plunges her into a deeper lassitude.

The seventh line asks: "Where is the loved one?" She does not see him. What she sees is only a vast stretch of grass that hides from her sight even the road that her husband should take when he returns. And this uncertainty about his homecoming increases the sadness of separation.

Since Confucius teaches moderation of feeling and expression, Chinese poets are rarely outspoken. As a result, the very essence of Chinese poetry is its power of suggestion. Chinese poets attach no importance to detailed description. Chinese poems are generally short, but in spite of their conciseness they are still long enough for a skilled poet to introduce, develop, embellish, and conclude his theme according to certain established rules. In a short poem, if a thousand details are intentionally omitted, the one that has the greatest power of suggestion is never neglected. As in a Sung painting, where a single brush stroke evokes a whole landscape; so does a single verse, a single image, express all the emotion of the poet. Chinese poets, unlike the Parnassians, are not painters of reality. They do not imitate nature but create a poetic world that invites our imagination to soar to infinity.

Thus, in order to understand Chinese poetry, one has to read meaning into the lines; or, according to a Chinese saying, one tries to listen to the sound that has ceased on the lyre, because often the Chinese poet does not dot his *i*'s but rather lets the reader do it, each according to his own fancy.

It has already been noted that Chinese poets do not impress us by the variety of their themes. However, Li Ch'ing-chao's subject matter is even more limited than that of others. Her scope of interest lies only in herself and her husband. From the didactic point of view, her works, therefore, are not marked by Confucianism. She does not consider poetry a means of moral instruction or of social comment. Her favorite and almost unique theme is love, esthetic or sensual; and she sometimes expresses herself with less moderation and discretion than the great Master would have recommended. That is why a certain critic has said in this regard that, of all the woman writers, Li Ch'ing-chao is the most shameless.

From the philosophical point of view, she is influenced by neither Taoism nor Buddhism. When Lao-tzu speaks of returning to nature, he means an overflowing of oneself into nature, a spiritual communion with nature in order to forget the self. Undoubtedly, Li Ch'ing-chao has a profound love for nature but in an entirely different sense. In her opinion, nature serves only as a beautiful setting for the easy flow of her verse. She does not forget herself because of surrounding natural beauty. On the contrary, she places herself in its center. She never writes as did the great T'ang poet Li Po in this quatrain:

Question and Answer in the Mountain

You ask me why I dwell in the green mountains.
Smiling, I reply not, heart in peace.
When fallen flowers are carried afar by the flowing water,
Methinks I am in another world and not among the mortals.

Nor does she write like the hermit-poet Szu K'ung-t'u:

The Natural*

Stoop, and there it is;
Seek it not right and left.
All roads lead thither,
One touch and you have the spring!
As though coming upon opening flowers,
As though gazing upon the new year,
Verily I will not snatch it,
Forced, it will dwindle away.
I will be like the hermit on the hill,
Like duckweed gathered on the stream,

* Translation by Herbert A. Giles, *A History of Chinese Literature*, p. 181.

And when emotions crowd upon me,
I will leave them to the harmonies of heaven.

When Li Ch'ing-chao describes natural scenery, she herself is
the central figure:

Modeled on P'in Ling*

Fallen flowers
Red as rouge;
Catkins softly flying;
The shooting of new bamboo;
Spring's affair.

Alone I sit in my inner chamber,
Facing a garden of tender leaves.
Over water and land hardly have I roamed,
His home-coming being too short.
In dreams I shall stroll with light steps
To the north of the city, by the meandering stream,
In whose icy ripples my eyes will lie mirrored for you.

From this poem, we can see that the first four lines furnish a
beautiful setting that serves only as a pretext for exalting "self."
From the sixth line on, she is always present, moving about in the
foreground so as to attract our attention constantly. It is early
spring; there are tender leaves, new bamboo shoots. When the
gentle breeze sweeps by, red flowers come tumbling to earth,
while willow flowers soar up into the air. A beauteous season! An
auspicious hour for promenade! But Chao Ming-ch'eng is again
absent, and the poetess is left alone pining for him. She then recalls that he has come back for awhile but has not stayed long
enough to roam with her to her heart's content on the lakes and
in the mountains. To make it up, she says, she will stroll in her
dream to the north of the city by the stream, her home town Chinan being a city of fountains and lakes, the water of which is as
limpid as a mirror.

In the following *tz'u*, she is even more self-centered than in the
preceding one. She is forever present, from the beginning to the
end:

* As the meaning of the title is unclear to me, it is left untranslated.

Modeled on *Painted Lips*

Alighting from the swing,
Languorously I trim my tiny, tiny hands.
Thin flowers loaded with heavy dewdrops,
Thin robe soaked with perspiration.

Beholding a visitor's approach,
Away I rush, bashful,
Wearing only stockings, gold hairpins slipping.
Yet back I turn in front of the door
To smell the green plums.

Having descended from the swing, her favorite sport, she trims her hands, white and small. She speaks of heavy dewdrops because it is early in the morning. But we do not know whether it is early or late spring, since thin flowers indicate either early spring, when few trees are in bloom, or late spring, when few flowers are left on the boughs. But that is not an important question. She talks about thin flowers loaded with heavy dewdrops only to compare them with her thin robe soaked with perspiration. Then somebody approaches unexpectedly. She feigns to rush away without putting on her shoes because a young lady is supposed to be shy. But she is born coquettish and cannot resist the temptation to look at the young man or to be looked at by him. So she turns back at the door and feigns to smell the green plums.

Li Ch'ing-chao is not at all influenced by Buddhist philosophy. Neither does she observe the principle of altruism which is extended even to the humblest animals, as does Han Yü who writes in the following poem:

Chase not the morning mosquito,
Spare the evening fly.
If they prove to be a nuisance,
Let a partition stop their flight.
Their life is ephemeral,
Let them have their small share like us.
The cool wind of the ninth moon
Will sweep them away with no trace left.

Nor does Li Ch'ing-chao express Buddhist philosophical ideas such as Po Chü-i does in the following poem:

The pine tree lives to a thousand years,
The hibiscus flower lasts a single day.
Both go to nothingness;
Why do we boast of our years and months?
P'eng Tzu distinguishes his death from ours,
But his is just the same.
Better learn not to appear,
Not to appear is also not to disappear.

The ideas expressed in the foregoing poem are representative of the Buddhist philosophy that consists in identifying life with death, one with ten thousand, reality with void. P'eng Tzu, a legendary personage referred to in the fifth line, is said to have lived eight hundred years. But from the Buddhist point of view, to die young and to die at the age of eight hundred are one and the same.

Nor does Li Ch'ing-chao write like Tu Fu, the great realist poet of the T'ang dynasty: "Wine and meat become stale within the vermilion gate,/Bones of those who died of cold lie on the road." Li Ch'ing-chao is not at all social-minded. She is pleasure-loving and aristocratic, not necessarily in a disparaging sense. In other words, she enjoys life. She has also experienced war, but her poetry never deals with warfare. Tu Fu, who has suffered cold and hunger because of war, regards it as the root of all evil:

An Ancient Battlefield

Descending from horseback on an ancient battlefield,
I look around: a vast stretch of emptiness.
The whining wind chases the floating clouds,
Yellow leaves fall in front of me.
In the anthills lie rotten bones,
Mingled with entangling grass.

Northern Expedition

Long did I wander amid the frontier dust.
Upon my return, my hair turned gray.
After a year's journeying, I came back to my thatched house.
My wife and my children were in rags;
The sighing pines seemed to cry bitterly with us in unison,

The flowing fountains mingled their sad murmuring with our
    sobs.
My beloved children with snow-white complexion turned
    away their faces to weep,
They were dirty and wore no stockings.

Such realism is never found in Li Ch'ing-chao's poetry. This is
the way in which she recalls the prosperous days of the Northern
Sung dynasty:

> When the Empire was prosperous,
> We ladies were much at leisure
> And valued highly the fifteenth day of each moon.
> Wearing coiffures adorned with emerald
> And gold-threaded, willowlike, snow-white belts,
> We rivaled one another in elegance.

On the contrary, when her contemporaries, such as Lu Yu and
General Yüeh Fei, picture in their memory the glorious days of
the Northern Sung Empire, their poems are animated by patriotism. Lu Yu: "The barbarians are not yet annihilated;/Autumn
has already come to my temples." Yüeh Fei wrote one of the most
beautiful poems ever inspired by the sentiment of patriotism:

Modeled on *The Whole River is Red*

From afar I behold the Central Plain.
Beyond the evening fog lie many a city and wall.
Nostalgically I recall the days of yore:
Flowers and willows protecting the Jade Arbor and Phoenix
    Pavilion,
Men and women in rich array,
Covered with pearls and emeralds,
Parading in front of Longevity Mount.
Yesterday the Fairy Palace echoed with songs and flutes,
Today iron hooves fill up the empire.
The air is filthy with dust.
Whither are our fellow countrymen?
They fill up the ditches.
Whither are our soldiers?
Their flesh greases the enemy sword.

A thousand villages have become wasteland
Though mountains and rivers remain.
When will the Emperor provide me a good army?
Whipping my horse, the river will I cross and purify.
Upon my return, I shall take a stroll in Hanyang,
As happy as the immortal who mounted a yellow crane.

But we should neither judge Li Ch'ing-chao's poetry from the moral point of view, nor blame her for not being patriotic, altruistic, or social-minded just because she does not write like Tu Fu or Yüeh Fei. The moralists make the mistake of confusing the motives and effects of poetry with poetry itself. While one may be motivated by moral, political, or social reasons to write a poem, these motives or themes alone will not make one a poet. Moreover, whatever our motives, the act of writing a poem is not a moral, political, or social act; it is an individual and creative act. Therefore, one should not judge poetry by non-artistic standards.

Similarly, poetry may exercise great influence on our moral, political, or social views; but such influence cannot determine its value as poetry. A reader has the right to object to a poem for moral, political, or social reasons; but he has no right to condemn it as a bad poem for the same reasons. As literary critics, we should only assess literary value; it is not our duty to relate a work of art to other systems of value.

An artist has the right to choose his subject matter and to handle it as he likes. What are really precious in an artist are his spontaneous feelings. Li Ch'ing-chao did not suffer from poverty and privation like Tu Fu, nor did she go to war like General Yüeh Fei. If she had tried to concern herself with social ideas or warfare, her poems would have been artificial and affected. She was true to herself: she wrote about what she felt and what she had experienced. Li Ch'ing-chao was purely an individualist and considered poetry as a means of self-expression. She was able to express her emotions and personality in poetic language, but her poetry lacks intellectual reflection. It is desirable that a poet have great sensitivity, but emotion alone is liable to lead to monotony, triviality, and superficiality.

As already pointed out, Li Ch'ing-chao placed herself in the center of her writings. Next came Chao Ming-ch'eng, for whom her love was inexpressibly profound. As a young bride, she wrote poems full of charm and coquetry:

Modeled on *Washing Brook Sand*

Smiling, I draw aside the hibiscus-colored bed curtains,
Place my perfumed cheeks against the duck-shaped incense
    burner.
Hardly have I turned my rippling eyes than he divines my
    thoughts.

Profound and tender is my love.
To a leaflet I confide my intimate thoughts:—
To invite him to renew love's affair when the flowers cast
    shadows in the moonlight.

Although Li Ch'ing-chao's marriage was arranged, she did feel
true love for her husband. That is why she sang prolifically of love
in its manifold phases: the ecstacy of love, the sorrows of separation, the yearning for the absent one, the torment of uncertainty,
the bliss of reunion, and the final despair of bereavement.

While Chao Ming-ch'eng was away, she was plunged into a per-
vasive lassitude:

Modeled on *The Beauteous Nien Nu*

Desolate is the courtyard.
Oblique wind, fine rain.
Doors should be shut.
The Cold Food Festival is nigh.
Adorable willows, coquettish flowers, unpleasant weather of
    all kinds.
Having composed a difficult poem,
Awakened from drowsiness caused by strong wine,
I feel particularly idle.
Wild geese all pass by,
Bearing not on their wings my thoughts for him.
For days, spring chilliness reigned in my pavilion,
With screens unrolled on every side.
I am too weary to lean against the jade balustrade.
My coverlet being chilled, the incense burnt out, I awaken
    from another dream,
Grieved, I cannot remain couched.
The dripping of clear morning dew,
The sprouting of new plane tree leaves,

What an auspicious hour for spring promenade!
Fog disappears when the sun is high.
I shall see if the day will be fine.

This poem depicts the poetess' solitude, lassitude, and longing for her beloved. The profundity of sadness is couched in very plain language. At the outset, wind and drizzle combine to create a world of desolation. The third line, "Doors should be shut," increases the sentiment of solitude, since the poetess is confined to the depth of her chamber, completely isolated from the outside world. With shut doors, the distance between her and the surroundings seems to widen.

Then she mentions the approach of the Cold Food Festival, suggesting that on festival days one is particularly inclined to think of those who are absent. Here she tells us that the weather is still more unpleasant with the approach of festival, in spite of the "adorable willows" and the "coquettish flowers."

In the sixth line, Li Ch'ing-chao speaks of escaping into oblivion through poetry and wine. But when she has finished writing, when tipsiness is gone, she feels particularly idle. The word *hsien*, which I have translated as "idle," has different meanings in Chinese poetry. Sometimes it implies a kind of philosophical contemplation, and does not mean just being unoccupied, but rather denotes a state of mind free from worldly cares and desires. But in this poem, the word "idle" has another connotation. Here it has no philosophical import; it signifies a nonchalant, listless, and wistful state of mind that resembles languor and ennui. This idle feeling is a kind of mood—subtle, elusive, intangible; and, at the same time, it is tinged with gentle melancholy. It is a kind of indefinable emotion, which could exist only in a highly cultured, aristocratic, and leisured society. While feeling idle, her thoughts are again with her absent husband, but she cannot ask the passing wild geese to bear them on their wings and convey them to the loved one, since birds are only insensitive creatures.

In the second stanza, the poetess says that for days the weather has been cold, so cold that she cannot roll up her bamboo screens. She no longer cares to lean against the balustrade to contemplate the landscape, and spends the endless days in seclusion. During the night, she cannot rest in peace but wanders from one dreamland to another. But when the coverlet is chilled, when incense is reduced to ashes, when she is awakened from another dream, she is so saddened that she must arise.

The morning scenes are most attractive: the dripping of dew-drops; the sprouting of the tender leaves of the plane tree. The day is meant for a spring promenade. But without company, she hesitates. So she says that she will wait to see if the day will be fine. If the day remains foggy, she will stay at home. But even if the sun chases away the fog, is she certain to go out for a stroll? No, the gloominess of her spiritual fog will prevent her from doing so.

In the following poem, the poetess contrasts her own indefinite separation from her husband with a mythical couple's happy annual reunion, so as to bring to light the hopelessness of her own situation. In order to have a correct understanding of the poem, we should first know the ancient legend of the Cowherd and the Spinning Maid. The Maid, who lived on the east side of the Milky Way, was a daughter of the Emperor of Heaven. Her work consisted in weaving cloudlike silk for making gorgeous celestial garments. Taking pity upon her loneliness, the Emperor of Heaven married her to the Cowherd on the west bank of the Milky Way. After the marriage, the love of the Spinning Maid for her husband was so profound that she neglected weaving and needlework. This irritated the Emperor of Heaven; he recalled the daughter from the west side of the Milky Way, giving her permission to meet her husband only once a year, on the night of the seventh day of the seventh moon. On that night, a group of magpies stretch out their wings to make a bridge over the Milky Way so that the celestial spouses can meet thereupon. That is why the night of the seventh day of the seventh moon is now bright, now gloomy, because at the hour of their meeting, the moon shines bright; when the sad hour of parting comes, the Spinning Maid sheds abundant tears; these are turned into raindrops, and the moon is dimmed thereby.

Modeled on *Hsing Hsiang Tzu* *

Frightened by the chirping of insects in the grass,
The leaves of the plane tree come tumbling to the ground.
Heavy are the sorrows up in the sky and here below.
So far away is the Moon Palace
And cloud perrons.

* As the meaning of this title is unclear to me, it is left untranslated.

22075

Thither we go not,
Even with rafts plying to and fro
Over the seas.

On the magpie bridge over the Milky Way,
The Cowherd and the Spinning Maid meet but once a year.
Eternal should be their sadness of parting.
Why is the night now fine, now rainy, now windy?
Is it the sad hour of farewell?

In the following poem, the word "separation" is never mentioned, but "sad dreams" suggest a continuous longing for her husband. And the poem is to be appreciated for its power of suggestion. It is late spring because the cuckoo is singing mournfully, deploring the dying of the glorious season. The wind has calmed down into tranquillity, but there are heaps of fallen petals, red and white, which create a sad atmosphere. The poetess declares that she always feels melancholy after the blooming of the begonias. In order to escape into oblivion, she resorts to wine and music, but they do not prevent her from having sad dreams.

Modeled on *The Happy Event is Nigh*

Calm is the wind, deep are the fallen flowers.
Heaps of rouge and snow on the other side of the screen.
After the blooming of the begonias
Melancholy comes the spring,
Ever do I recall.

Wine is drunk, songs are sung, the jade cup is empty.
The lamp is now dim, now bright.
Sad enough are my dreams;
How can I still bear the mournful notes of the cuckoo?

Solitude and sadness form the woof and warp of this poem, which, like the preceding one, is also full of imagery:

Modeled on *The Moon Shines Upon the Pear Flowers*

Late spring in the imperial city . . .
Double doors, courtyard profound.
Grass is green up to my perrons.

> No wild geese crossing the nocturnal sky,
> Who bears my letter afar?
> Skeins of sorrows.
>
> A tender soul is forever amorous.
> Indifference is no easy affair.
> Here again is the Cold Food Festival.
> Motionless is the swing, silent is the street.
> The moon casts its rays athwart
> And soaks the pear blossoms.

In the second line, "double doors" and "courtyard profound" give us an idea of isolation. The next line suggests that nobody has come to see the lonely poetess, because the grass has not been trodden black by footsteps. Then the thoughts of Li Ch'ing-chao are again with Chao Ming-ch'eng. She complains that she cannot even ask the wild geese to convey her thoughts to her husband, since there are no wild geese passing through the nocturnal sky. Once more, sorrows are likened to skeins of sorrows binding her tender heart, which cannot remain indifferent, especially on festival days. The last three verses form a beautiful setting. It is a silent night. The swing is motionless; human voices in the street are stilled. Only the soft and glistening moonbeams, comparable to water, soak the pear flowers.

This poem was written in Li Ch'ing-chao's widowhood, probably not soon after Chao Ming-ch'eng's death, because the anguish expressed here is not so violent as that revealed in the *tz'u* entitled *Promenade in the Royal Street*:

Modeled on *Nan Ke Tzu* *

> High up, the Milky Way is shimmering,
> Here below my curtains are drooping.
> Coolness is born on my pillow soaked with tears.
> Getting up to undress myself,
> I wonder how advanced is the night.
>
> Small are the emerald envelopes of the lotus seeds,
> Few are the lotus leaves of gold.
> The same weather and robe as before,
> Only my heart is not as of yore.

* As the meaning of this title is unclear to me, it is left untranslated.

It is an autumn night. Our poetess, who has first gone to bed without undressing, awakens late at night, gets up to undress, and wonders what time it is. The first two lines of the second stanza are a vivid picture of autumn: the lotus leaves have turned yellow and are few, the green envelopes of the lotus seeds are still small. While undressing, Li Ch'ing-chao pictures in her memory the happy days of old and says that autumn is the same, her robe is the same, but her heart is no longer the same.

The poems cited in this chapter afford ample evidence that Li Ch'ing-chao is a pure poet but not a great thinker.

VI *Poetess as a Critic*

As I have already mentioned, Li Ch'ing-chao did not develop any theory of art. However, she did write a very short essay on *tz'u*. As she began this essay by mentioning *Yüeh Fu,* it is necessary to comment on it. The *Yüeh Fu,* or Department of Music, originated with Emperor Wu (reigned 140–87 B.C.) of the Western Han dynasty. This brilliant Emperor, after having driven the Huns to Central Asia, entered into an alliance with Tibet and Turkestan, extended the Chinese frontiers to Annam, and opened an epoch highly favorable for the development of art and literature. Emperor Wu not only enthusiastically patronized literature but also devoted great attention to music. He established the *Yüeh Fu,* or Department of Music, which was charged with the task of collecting, transcribing, editing, and preserving the folk songs of the empire, as well as those of its neighbors. A contemporary of his called Mei Ch'eng (d. 140 B.C.) had the honor of being the first to bring home from the non-Chinese world the five-word meter, while the Emperor himself was the first to compose a poem of all seven-syllabic lines. Up to then, Chinese poems were still composed on the style of *The Book of Odes* or *The Poems of Ch'u.*

Later, men of letters began to write poems in the manner of the *Yüeh Fu* songs. Thus the term *yüeh fu* came to denote not only the Department of Music, but also poems written in the manner of the folk songs collected by it. Metrically speaking, the *yüeh fu* songs approximate those of ancient verse, with the difference being that only the former was set to music. Like *tz'u, yüeh fu* is also meant for singing. So it can be said that *yüeh fu* is the direct ancestor of *tz'u,* with the difference being that, in the case of *tz'u* the rules of versification are more complicated.

The *yüeh fu* poems are usually composed of verses of equal length, pentasyllabic or heptasyllabic. The number of lines is indefinite, and there is no fixed tone pattern. Rhyme occurs at the end of the even-numbered lines; one can use one rhyme throughout, or vary it. Prosodically, the construction of *tz'u* is much more complicated than that of the poems of *yüeh fu,* since each tune has a separate tone pattern and rhyme scheme of its own. Some liberty is allowed regarding the arrangement of subtones, but the rhyme scheme must be strictly observed. As Li Ch'ing-chao was also a great phonetician and musician, she was very exacting about tone pattern. The reason she attached great importance to tone pattern is not only because different tones produce different auditory effects, but also because they express different feeling. It is said that flat tones express moderate feeling, while sharp tones express violent passion.

In her essay on *tz'u,* Li Ch'ing-chao began by saying that *yüeh fu* attained its highest glory during the reign of Emperor Hsüan Tsung of the T'ang dynasty, who founded the Garden of Pear Blossoms for training young boys and girls in the art of music. She noted that the best singer of that period was Li the Eighth. One day, she continued, a high-ranking official entertained some guests at a feast. Among them was a young scholar who asked Li the Eighth to put on a poor man's clothes and go to the feast incognito. He introduced the disguised Li the Eighth as his cousin without mentioning that Li was a singer.

At the feast, the food was rich, the wine abundant, and the music exquisite. A singer called Ts'ao Yüan-Ch'ien sang a song called "The Beauteous Nien Nu" and won everyone's admiration. The young scholar suddenly pointed to Li the Eighth and asked him: "Will you also sing for us, my dear cousin?" Those who were present looked at him disdainfully. But as soon as he opened his mouth, they were moved to tears. The young scholar then revealed that the singer was Li the Eighth.

Later, songs of the states of Cheng and Wei came into vogue, and new tunes were also created. Melodies such as "Buddhist Coiffure," "Beautiful Spring," "Washing Brook Sand," "Dreaming of the South Bank and Fisherman" enjoyed a great fame. Then, during the chaotic period of the Five Dynasties (907–960), literature was on the decline. However, the second king of Nan T'ang (Southern T'ang) and his son, the last king of the dynasty, were highly cultured. The former wrote immortal verse, such as:

Gone is the perfume of the lotus flowers, withered are their
    leaves of emerald.
From the green waves, melancholy rises with the west wind.

But his poems were so sad that they betrayed the thoughts of a
sovereign predestined to lose his kingdom.

The Sung dynasty is remarkable for its literary as well as military achievements, and deserves to be placed in the first rank
among builders of civilization. More than a hundred years after
the establishment of the dynasty, Liu Yung composed new melodies and wrote new types of *tz'u* for them. He published a collection of songs and his fame became widespread. Although his
verses were harmonious, his language was vulgar. Chang Tzu-yeh,
the Sung brothers, Shen T'ang, Yüan Chiang, and Ts'ao Tz'u-ying
also managed to write astonishing verses now and then, but on the
whole they do not deserve to be called great poets.

Yen Yüan-hsien, Ou-Yang Yung-shu, and Su Tzu-chan were
talented scholars but their poems were not suitable for singing.
Why? Because they ignored the fact that, in writing an ordinary
poem, the poet has only to distinguish flat tones from sharp tones;
but, in writing a *tz'u,* he also has to pay attention to the five subtones, the rhythm and the variation in stress. For instance, in such
songs as "Andante" and "Flowers in the Rain," one may use flat
rhyme as well as sharp rhyme. In the melody "Spring in the Jade
Pavilion," one may use any of the five tones at the end of the
rhymed lines. But if one uses the fifth tone, then the *tz'u* will not
be suitable for singing.

Li Ch'ing-chao concluded her essay with these comments about
her contemporaries. "The prose of Tseng Tzu-ku and Wang
Chieh-fu is comparable to that of the writers of the Western Han
dynasty, but their *tz'u* is ridiculous." Thus she affirmed that the
composition of *tz'u* was a special art, which few could really master. From this essay on *tz'u* we can also gather that Li Ch'ing-
chao possessed little humility and was very severe towards her
contemporaries:

"Yen Shu-yüan, Ho Fang-huei, Ch'in Shao-yu, and Huang Lu-
chih were initiated into the mystery of *tz'u* writing. However,
Yen's *tz'u* is poor in description, that of Ho lacks substance, and
Ch'in's is rich in sensitivity but lacking in sobriety of language.
Therefore Ch'in's *tz'u* is like a beautiful woman from a poor fam-
ily, good-looking without being majestic. Huang's poetry, sober

but full of weak points, can be likened to a piece of jade, of good quality but not flawless.

VII *The Minor Poems*

Many Chinese poets are fond of using allusion in their writings. An allusion is a proper noun or a ready-made expression referring to a past event and is employed to present a situation—either to draw an analogy between a past event and the present situation in the poem, or to provide a contrast between them. Allusion is used as an economical means of presenting a situation; it is a sort of shorthand device that tells the reader certain stories or facts that would otherwise require detailed explanation and take up space. For instance, the term "the one who plays on the flute" is now currently employed to denote a husband, because it refers to Hsiao Shih, who perfectly imitated the singing of the phoenix on his instrument, and who, with his wife, was borne away by a phoenix one day to fairyland.

A. SUGGESTIVE DESCRIPTIVE

The following *tz'u* of Li Ch'ing-chao is an ode to white chrysanthemums. As it abounds in allusion with commentary, it seems unintelligible to non-Chinese. Moreover, this *tz'u* is unusual for this reason.

Modeled on *Beauties*

Chilled is my pavilion,
With screens drooping during the endless night.
I loathe the merciless wind and rain.
Spoiling the jade skin of the white chrysanthemums.
They resemble not the rosy cheeks of the Precious Consort
    in tipsiness,

Nor the frowning Sun Shou.
Neither the perfume stolen by Han Shou
Nor the powdered face of Lady Hsü
Are comparable to them.
Viewed with minuteness,
They have the air of Ch'ü P'ing and Magistrate T'ao.
When the gentle breeze sweeps by,
Their friendly scent is similar to that of T'u Mi.

Autumn is dying.
Their whiteness evocative of snow and jade
Is pure but lean.
They seem full of sadness,
Like the young lady who removed her jade ornament in
    Hankao,
Or the one who, tearful, wrote a poem on a silk fan.
Now the moon is bright and the breeze gentle,
Now the day is gloomy with rain and heavy fog.
It is Heaven's will that they wither.

In spite of my love for them,
I know not how long their lives will span.
Enamored as I am of them,
They need not envy the river bank or the east hedge.

From the fifth line onward this poem is filled with proper
nouns referring to historical personages.

In the fifth line, the poetess suggests that the beauty of the
white chrysanthemum is superior to that of the Precious Consort,
a historical beauty and the favorite of Emperor Hsüan Tsung of
the T'ang dynasty. The Emperor was so enthralled by her charms
that he ceased to concern himself with state affairs; this led to
the outbreak of a serious rebellion. Sun Shou, the great beauty,
liked to frown, and frowning enhanced her charms. Here the
poetess points out that the loveliness of Sun Shou is inferior to
that of the white chrysanthemums.

In the seventh and eighth lines, the poetess suggests that the
sweet scent of the white chrysanthemums is incomparable. It is
superior to the perfume stolen by Han Shou and to the powder of
Lady Hsü. Han Shou, a handsome young man of the third century who lived under the Chin dynasty, was the aide-de-camp
to Prime Minister Chia Ch'ung, whose daughter fell in love with
him. She received from him a rare perfume, which he had stolen
from his master, who had received it from the Emperor as a gift.
When the father discovered their secret love, he was obliged to
let her marry Han Shou. Lady Hsü was a concubine of Emperor
Yüan of the Liang dynasty. She committed adultery with a cour-
tier named Chi Chiang, who remarked with a sigh: "In spite of
her age, Lady Hsü is still beautiful and amorous."

Then in line eleven, our poetess carefully scrutinizes the chrysanthemums and thinks that only the nobility of the soul of Ch'ü P'ing or Magistrate T'ao is comparable to them. Ch'ü P'ing, or Ch'ü Yüan, a loyal minister of King Huai of the Ch'u State of the feudal period, enjoyed the full confidence of his king until the jealousies and intrigues of his rivals weakened his position at court. In exile, he composed the famous long poem entitled *Li Sao* (Falling into Trouble), in which he compared the superior man to aromatic herbs and odorous flowers. He particularly loved chrysanthemums for their perfume and purity and took them as a symbol of the soul's nobility. He said in *Li Sao:* "In the evening, I savor the withered petals of the chrysanthemums."

Magistrate T'ao in the same line refers to T'ao Ch'ien, or T'ao Yüan-ming, another poet enamored of chrysanthemums. After a youth of poverty, he finally obtained an appointment as magistrate. But he was unfitted for official life. He held the post for merely eighty-three days, because he objected to receiving a superior officer with the usual ceremonious bowing on the ground. He "could not crook the hinges of my back for five packs of rice." He then retired to private life and busied himself with poetry, music, drinking, and the cultivation of flowers, especially chrysanthemums, which became closely associated with his name. Two of his famous lines read: "Plucking the chrysanthemums near the east hedge,/I behold the South Hill which appears peaceful and tranquil."

In the second stanza, Li Ch'ing-chao declares that at the end of autumn, chrysanthemums become thinner and look very sad, so sad that they may be likened to the young lady who removed her jade ornament in Hankao or to the lady who wrote a poem on a silk fan. Hankao is the ancient name for Hankow. According to a collection of fairy tales, a certain young man named Cheng Chiao-fu there met a beautiful girl with whom he fell in love at first sight. The girl, who was an immortal, removed a jade ornament attached to her robe and presented it to him as a gift. Then they walked on. After a few steps, both the jade ornament and the girl disappeared altogether.

The one who wrote a poem on a silk fan was Pan Chieh-yü, for a long time a favorite concubine of Emperor Ch'eng of the Eastern Han dynasty. When she was supplanted afterwards by a younger and more beautiful rival, she presented to the Emperor a silk fan on which was inscribed the following poem:

Plaintive Song

I tore off a piece of Shantung silk
As white as frost and snow.
I cut it to make a fan
As round as the moon.
It will be a close companion of thee,
Its movement producing a gentle breeze.
Often it fears the approach of autumn,
When cold wind will sweep away the dying summer's heat.
It will then be abandoned in a bamboo chest,
Losing your love and favor.

The allusion to the lady's removing her jade ornament and to Pan Chieh-yü's plaintive song suggest that at the end of autumn, the chrysanthemums, foreseeing their tragic end, seem so sad that they may be likened to the fairy who regretted the impossible love affair between an immortal and a mortal, or to Lady Pan Chieh-yü, who fell into disgrace with her imperial lover.

In the last verse, "river bank" again refers to Ch'ü Yüan, who in his exile wandered along the river bank, and "east hedge" refers to T'ao Ch'ien's planting chrysanthemums there. The poetess concludes that she loves chrysanthemums so much that they should envy neither the friendship of Ch'ü Yüan nor that of T'ao Ch'ien.

Another *tz'u* highly appreciated also for its suggestive power is the following:

Modeled on Washing Brook Sand

Let not the deep cup be filled with rich and amber-colored
    wine;
Languor seizes me before drunkenness.
Bells have already echoed in the evening wind.

The scent of incense is gone, so is my dream.
My hairpins of "cold-proof gold" being too small, my coiffure
    is undone.
Awakening, I am facing only the red flowers of the candles.

In the first stanza, the poetess tells us that she does not want her cup filled with strong wine because she will be amorously languid before getting drunk, suggesting that she is afraid of feeling amorous since Chao Ming-ch'eng is absent from home. The day is dying; bells have already echoed in the evening wind; and our poetess lights the incense before going to bed. The incense will keep burning throughout the night, being extinguished by daybreak. After getting up at daybreak, the poetess lights a pair of red candles whose flames are likened to flowers. In front of the mirror, she combs her hair because the coiffure is undone, her hairpins made of "cold-proof gold" being too small to keep it tight. But a word should be said about "cold-proof gold." During the reign of Emperor Ming of the Wei dynasty, the state of Annam presented to the sovereign a bird that spit forth gold. As the tropical bird was very much afraid of cold weather, the Emperor had a small house built for it, called "Cold-Proof Pavilion." The gold spit by the bird, called "cold-proof gold," was used to make hairpins for the ladies of the harem.

In the second stanza, the poetess tells us that after waking up, she faces only the red flowers of the candles. This remark, apparently simple and plain, has a hidden sense. Red candles are usually lit in the nuptial chamber; but in the poem she faces the red candles without her spouse.

This *tz'u*, also rich in suggestion, indicates regret over the dying spring, weariness, idleness, chilliness:

Modeled on *Washing Brook Sand*

Grieved by the dying spring, I am too weary to trim my coiffure.
In the courtyard, the evening wind sweeps the plum flowers
    to earth.
Light clouds go to and fro, the moon is dimmed.

Incense lying idle in the duck-shaped jade burner,
The fringes of the cherry-colored bed curtains drooping.
Will the *t'ung hsi* plant still be cold-proof?

In the first stanza, it is a beautiful night of late spring, one of moonlight, shadows, and fallen petals. Grieved by the dying of spring and the absence of her husband, the poetess feels too weary to comb her hair, and the inanimate things around seem weary too: incense lying idle in the burner; fringes of the cherry-colored bed curtains idly drooping. In the second stanza, in order to suggest chilliness, the poetess speaks of a cold-proof plant called *t'ung hsi*. According to a legend about the T'ang, the state of

Annam once presented to a Chinese emperor a plant called *t'ung hsi*. The gold-colored plant was placed in a golden plate. It was winter, and the plant exuded a very pleasant warmth. The envoy told the Emperor that it was a cold-proof plant.

Another *tz'u* to the red plum blossom is highly appreciated for its minute description. In ancient China, plum trees were usually planted on the stream bank so that their graceful branches might be reflected in the water. That is why poets, when writing about plum blossoms, not only depict the flowers themselves but also the graceful shadows of the twigs in the water. The adjective "thin" is always associated with plum branches, because when the tree is in bloom, few leaves remain on the boughs.

In the fourth line of the second stanza, Princess Shou Yang, daughter of a Sung emperor, is mentioned because of her plum blossom-adorned coiffure. One spring day, she was slumbering in front of the Han Chang Palace under the eaves when plum flowers fell on her temple. She then started the fashion of a plum blossom-adorned coiffure, which came to be imitated by all young women, whether rich or poor. In the next-to-last line, the flute is called a "barbarian" flute because it is an imported instrument. A famous ancient air *Fallen Plum Flowers,* is played on the flute; that is why in poetry it is often associated with dying plum flowers.

Modeled on *New Jade Candle*

After the twelfth moon on the stream bank,
A few red plum blossoms
Are seen well-cut and delicately wrought.
The tender flowers, as smooth as jade,
Slightly reveal the glory of spring.
I well imagine the shadows of their slantwise twigs
Rich in perfume impregnating the sleeves,
Flung by the moonbeams last evening
On the silent stream bank
In the front village.

Facing the wine cup,
I ask my talented companion
If he knows the spring glory beyond the hills.
The plum blossom-adorned coiffure of Princess Shou Yang

Is no equal to a thin water-reflected twig.
Gentle is the breeze, fine the rain.
In luxuriance and disorder grow the flowers.
Yet trust the mercilessness of the barbarian flute
Which is piping forth a mournful note.

B. INNER AND OUTER SCENES

In many of her poems, Li Ch'ing-chao presents vivid pictures of spring. In the following poem, the first stanza deals with inner scenes, the second with outer ones; but both are endowed with a pathetic beauty. In the first line, the employment of the word "idle" to qualify the word "casement" is an ingenious device; in the second stanza, the verbs "urge" and "play" are also unusual:

Modeled on *Washing Brook Sand*

Through the idle casement, I behold the remnants of spring in the small courtyard.
The screen being unrolled, heavy are the shadows.
In my elevated abode, speechless, I play my jade lute.

Clouds soaring above the distant hills urge the twilight,
The gentle breeze blowing the drizzling rain plays with light shadows.
Inevitably, the pear flowers are dying.

And, as the following discussion and quotations will illustrate, Li Ch'ing-chao often used the seasons to express grief, aloneness, and the transient quality of life. In this poem, Li Ch'ing-chao, sensitive to time, expresses most subtly regret over its irretrievable passing:

Modeled on *Washing Brook Sand*

All above my elevated abode, hangs the sunny blue sky,
In front of my elevated abode, green grasses spread to the horizon;
Do not ascend to the top of the staircase.

The new shoots have already grown into bamboo beneath the perrons;
The fallen flowers have all gone into the nests of the swallows.
I cannot bear to hear beyond the woods the song of the cuckoo.

In the first stanza, the luxuriance of grass that stretches to the horizon suggests the passing of spring. At the same time, it also suggests longing for her absent husband, because green grass is closely associated with two famous verses of the great T'ang poet Wang Wei: "Spring grass will turn green in the coming year;/ Will the noble young man then return home?" That is why in the next line the poetess warns herself not to ascend the top floor because, even if she tries to look afar, all that she will see will be green grass, but no trace of her loved one.

The second stanza begins with an antithetical couplet: "New shoots have already grown into bamboo beneath the perrons;/ Fallen petals have all gone into the nests of the swallows." An antithetical couplet is two lines of parallel construction that contrast in sense as well as in tone. Just like allusion and symbolism, antithesis is also an important and characteristic poetic device in Chinese. When abused, it becomes an artificial pairing of words. In this *tz'u*, the antithetical couplet is natural and skilful.

In the last line, the cry of the cuckoo is associated with unhappy love because of an ancient legend. An emperor of Shu who fell in love with the wife of one of his ministers was transformed into a cuckoo after his death. The cuckoo's cry is supposed to sound like *Pu ju kuei* (It is better to return home). In the poem, the cry of the cuckoo becomes a plea on behalf of the poetess to her absent husband.

And the following *tz'u*, one written in her old age and probably during her period of exile to Chinhua in Chekiang, expresses the desolation of one nearing the end of time:

Modeled on *Joy of Peace*

Year after year, in the snow,
Tipsy, I stuck plum blossoms in my hair.
Caressing them, I am no less disheartened,
My robe is fully stained with tears.

This year, I am at the corner of the sea and at the sky's limit.
My temples have turned grey.
Owing to the violence of the evening wind,
'Tis hardly possible to contemplate the plum flowers.

And, in another *tz'u*, the atmosphere of desolation reigns from beginning to end:

Modeled on *Thinking of Lady Ch'in*

I mount the high pavilion.
Mountains in disorder, vast countryside, thin mist,
Thin mist.
After the crows return homeward to perch,
Horns are heard in the evening air.

Incense is burned to ash, tipsiness is gone, sad is my heart.
Plane tree leaves come tumbling down to earth,*
Plane tree leaves come tumbling down to earth,
Once again the beauteous pall of autumn,
Once again the feeling of solitude.

To begin with, the poetess unfolds a scene like a scroll of
Chinese painting, and our eyes move from one object to another:
the scattered mountains, the vast countryside enveloped in a thin
layer of mist. A sad sight! Then comes the sound of the moaning
crows and the evening horns. A sad sound!

In the second stanza, the line "Incense is burned to ash" indicates the lapse of time. In ancient China, one lit incense before
going to bed. It kept burning through the night and was extinguished at daybreak. It is now morning, since the incense has
burned to ash. Awake with the effect of the wine having worn off,
the poetess is lucid. The morning scene is as sad as the evening
one because in front of her lie the fallen leaves of the plane tree,
and the withering of autumn leaves is liable to call forth such sad
images as the onset of old age and death.

Another *tz'u* deals with homesickness but at the same time dis-
plays a keen awareness of time:

Modeled on *Unburdening Oneself*

This night, heavily drunk, I fell into slumber with make-up
     undone.
The plum blossoms were still in my hair,
Their perfume chased away my tipsiness and drowsiness.
My dream being broken, I failed to return home.

Voices are stilled,
Fair is the moon,

* Two words missing in the original text.

Unrolled is my emerald screen.
I caress the dying blossoms
And savor the remnants of their perfume,
While time glides by.

In the first stanza, the poetess manifests her wish to go home in dreams, but the perfume of the plum blossoms in her hair is so strong that it awakens her and makes her dreams disappear. In the second, the poetess laments the fading away of the plum blossoms, regretfully caresses them, and savors the remnants of their perfume, while the dying blossoms and the gliding of time arouse her apprehension over the passing away of her own youth.

The whole life of Li Ch'ing-chao was successful, and her poems are the result thereof. By this statement, I do not mean that she knew only happiness but that she was capable of living many moments intensely. She regarded everything poetically and philosophically, she beautified adversity as well as fortune. In the poem that follows, she still retains in sickness, solitude, and old age, a state of mind free from worry and desire. All the surrounding objects, from the boiling medicine pot to the landscape in the rain and the cassia flower, seem as calm and peaceful as her own mind. There is no regret over her illness, nor is there any suggestion of sadness. The idleness she feels in her sickbed is raised to the level of philosophical and esthetic contemplation.

Modeled on *A New Version of Washing Brook Sand*

In convalescence, my temples have turned gray.
Lying on the couch, I watch the sinking moon climb up the
    muslin-veiled casement.
The cardamom is boiling in hot water,
Not the tea leaves.

Lying idly against my pillow, I write excellent verse,
Outdoor scenes are fairer in the rain.
All day long the cassia flower turns itself to me,
So lovingly.

C. LOVE, LONELINESS

In the minor poems that follow we find once more the familiar *kuei*, the most fragrant of flowers, and the pictures of spring and of other scenes. But most of them are used to express the poetess' love for her husband and her loneliness when he is absent. Among these poems, there are also some that celebrate special circumstances and some that celebrate hero worship. In the following poem, we have an ode to the *kuei:*

Modeled on *Partridges in the Sky*

Slightly yellow, infinitely dainty.
Their hearts seem distant, only the perfume is nigh.
Though without leaves of tender green nor blossoms of deep red,
Yet they reign supreme among flowers.

Surely they make the plum blossoms jealous
And the chrysanthemums shy.
They are the first to open at the mid-autumn festival near the
    painted railings.
Were men of letters of yore insensitive?
Why were they so thoughtless about them?

In another *tz'u,* addressed to her husband who often spent the wondrous spring season away from home, the first three lines depict the glories of spring: green grass, half-open plum blossoms. But suddenly clouds gather and soon the plum blossoms are swept by the wind and rain down to earth, mingled with dust. Confronted with this sad spectacle, the poetess says that she prefers sleeping to drowning her sadness in a cup of wine. But the evening turns out to be a beautiful one, and the first two lines of the second stanza are really a thing of beauty. In the last three lines, the poetess expresses her loneliness and her desire to share the spring with her husband:

Modeled on *Small Hills*

Spring has come to my door, green grows the grass of spring.
Plum blossoms are slightly broken,
Not yet in full bloom.
But clouds are gathering
And the jade buds are smashed to dust.
Fain would I prefer a morning dream
To my cup of wine.

Double doors loaded with flower shadows,
Grossly-plaited screens spread with pale moon,
What a beauteous evening!

Twice in three years you missed the spring.
Do come back—
Let's enjoy this one to our hearts' content.

In another *tz'u*, addressed to Chao Ming-ch'eng on his leaving
for Laichow to assume the duties of a magistrate, the poetess refers in the first stanza to *Yang-Kuan*, the name of an ancient farewell song. And this reference is appropriate for she has accompanied her husband to an inn where she has many times sung the
song and drunk with him in order to forget the sorrows of separation. In the second stanza, Tunglai is the ancient name for Laichow; and P'englai, the dwelling of Taoist immortals, is associated with two verses of the famous T'ang poet Li Shang-yin:
"P'englai lies at no great distance,/May the Bluebird eagerly
convey to her my tender thoughts." The *tz'u* by Li Ch'ing-chao:

Modeled on *Butterflies Enamored of Flowers*

My silk robe is soaked with tears mingled with powder and rouge,
A thousand times have I sung the refrain of *Yang Kuan*.
Mountains are said to be endless but an end there is;
The drizzling rain is heard in the silent inn.

Troubled is my heart by the sadness of parting.
At the hour of farewell,
I forget whether the cup was filled to the brim.
With luck, I can count on wild geese to bear my letters,
Tunglai being not so far as P'englai.

In the following ode to plum blossoms, Li Ch'ing-chao's favorite flower which she so often wrote about, it is again spring and
the plum flowers that herald this season are in bloom. But she is
alone: Chao Ming-ch'eng is absent; her friends seem to have for-
gotten her. She feels so lonely that she likens herself to Ho Sun, a
solitary poet of the Liang dynasty who also loved plum blossoms.

Modeled on *A Garden Full of Flowers*

Spring is hidden in my pavilion,
Daylight locked within my idle casement.
Infinitely profound is my painted hall.
Incense is burned to ashes,
Sunlight has climbed down the hooks of my curtains.

The plum tree I have planted being in bloom,
Need I still roam the mountains or the waters?
No visitors,
I am as lonely as Ho Sun in Yangchow.
I know that the plum flowers
Fear to be marred
By wind and rain.
Whose flute
Pipes forth a mournful sound?
Loathe not the withered plum flowers,
Trust that their spirit remains even when they are swept away
    without trace.
Words suffice not to tell
Even the grace of the stripped boughs
In the moonlight on a beauteous night.

In another *tz'u*—one doubtless written shortly after her marriage—Li Ch'ing-chao, young and elegant, wears a bird-shaped
gold hairpin and a glistening silk robe. The buckle of her belt is
heart-shaped, the symbol of undying love. Under the closed,
hibiscus-colored bed curtains, she has probably spent a *nuit
blanche*, and that is why she has stained her robe with powder-
mingled tears and not undone the buckle of her belt:

Modeled on *Buddhist Coiffure*

A gold bird soaring above my cloudlike coiffure,
My eyebrows frowning upon the thin spring mist,
Closed hibiscus-colored bed curtains within my pavilion,
Superimposed hills on my painted screen.

Through the icy casement I behold the daybreak.
The heart-shaped buckle of my belt remains undone.
I have stained my silk robe with tears mingled with powder,
Wondering when my loved one will return home.

Or we have the following *tz'u*, which was probably written in
Nanking during the absence of Chao Ming-ch'eng; for the Purple Mountain mentioned in the poem is a famous scenic spot of
this city:

Modeled on *Water Washes Away the Sand*

At daybreak, beyond my screen,
Wind blew away my dream with no trace left.
Who will accompany me when I mount again the painted
    pavilion?
I have stirred the fire with my jade hairpin, I still recall,
Incense is burned to ashes.

Turning back I behold the Purple Mountain,
Soaked with rain, wrapped in heavy mist.
The waves of the spring river are now slumbering,
Only yesterday's tears are left on my silk robe,
I shed them to the wild geese when they passed by.

Awakening from a dream in which Chao Ming-ch'eng was
mounting the painted pavilion in her company, she realizes that
he is absent. So she asks: "Who will accompany me when I mount
again the painted pavilion?" She then recalls that she has stirred
the incense with her jade hairpin before going to bed, but that
now the incense is burned out. This is a subtle way to indicate
the lapse of time.

She then beholds the Purple Mountain looming dark in the distance, sodden with rain and enveloped in a thin layer of fog, and
the river whose waves are now calmed, now agitated. But instead
of using the words "calmed" and "agitated," she employs the
words "slumbering" and "awake." Again her thoughts are with
her husband. She says that only yesterday's tears are still left on
her silk dress and that they were shed when the wild geese were
passing by. In Chinese poetry, the wild goose symbolizes travel
and is associated with one who is absent from home. That is why
when the wild geese pass by they always remind Li Ch'ing-chao
of her husband's absence.

In the following farewell poem to Chao Ming-ch'eng, "my family of salt and catkins" in the second stanza refers to the family
of scholar Hsieh An of the Chin dynasty. One day he was teaching his daughter Hsieh Tao-yün to compose poetry when suddenly it began to snow. He jokingly asked: "What can the falling
snow be likened to?" His nephew Hsieh Lang answered: "It can
be likened to salt spread in the air." But his daughter answered:
"It is like willow flowers flying in the wind." By alluding to cat-

kins, Li Ch'ing-chao suggests that she herself is as talented as Hsieh Tao-yün, who compared the falling snow to willow flowers flying in the air when the breeze sweeps by. If she had not used an allusion but simply written: "I used to be praised for my talent," she would have appeared conceited.

Modeled on *Black Jade Table*

On the road to Hantan, no steed is seen.
Hasten not your departure!
How am I to spend the desolate windy autumn
Drinking together by the lit casement
And whispering under the dim lamplight
Are the things to be regretted most.

Each of us is grieved by reunion's brevity,
When new poems and astonishing verses are composed.
I used to be praised for my family of salt and catkins,
Today my beauty has begun to fade.
Only tears are left to me,
As abundant as yellow plum rain.

In the absence of Chao Ming-ch'eng, Li Ch'ing-chao entertained some friends at a banquet to celebrate the blooming of the plum tree in her back garden. This *tz'u* was written on that occasion:

Modeled on *Enamored of Her Charms*

Few are the jade flowers, rich is the perfume.
Snow has melted away from the branches.
Alas! This year, again, belated is my visit to the plum blossoms,
Clouds and water separate my riverside pavilion and his Ch'u
    abode.
Long and chilly is the day,
I lean against the railings with screen slightly up-rolled.

Guests have arrived,
Goblets are filled,
Our songs mingle with the passing water and clouds.
The south branch is ready for plucking.
Await not the sound of the barbarian flute
From the west pavillion.

And the following poem of circumstance was written during the spring festival when Li Ch'ing-chao entertained some relatives at a banquet:

Modeled on *Butterflies Enamored of Flowers*

All the lengthy night I have been feeling cheerless;
In vain have I dreamed of Ch'ang-an and recognized the road
    thereto.
Beauteous is the spring this year,
The glow of flowers and the moonlight rival each other.

Though cups and dishes are hastily prepared,
The wine is excellent and the plums are acid,
Pleasant to the taste.
Oh, flowers that I stuck into my hair in tipsiness, laugh not at me!
Alas! I am growing old just as the spring.

In still another poem of separation, spring has come; and Chao Ming-ch'eng is not at home to drink with his wife or to echo her poems. She leans against her pillow, but her great sorrow prevents slumber. So she trims the lamp wick, for an ancient tradition says that, when the burnt end of the wick forms a double-headed flower, the lovers will soon be reunited:

Modeled on *Butterflies Enamored of Flowers*

Warm rain, fair wind, the thaw has set in.
From the eyes of the willows and the cheeks of the plum flowers,
Spring is seen stirring.
Who shares with me poetry and wine?
Tears mingled with powder weigh heavily on my temple orna-
    ments.
Wearing my gold-threaded, lined robe,
I lean against my hill-shaped pillow,
My phoenix hairpin is damaged thereby.
Lonely and full of sorrow, sweet dreams I dream not,
Still do I trim the burnt end of the lampwick, though night is
    no longer young.

In another ode to the plum flower, the blossom she uses to ex-press her longing for her absent husband, Li Ch'ing-chao speaks in the first stanza of the tardy spring and of the belated blooming of the plum flower. The first line of this stanza denotes the lapse of time. The plum flowers have already become thinner, and the branches are no longer heavy with blossoms. But Chao Ming-ch'eng, absent, does not know that the rich perfume is gone; he will come back only when the almond tree will be in bloom.

Modeled on *Fairies on the River Bank*

Profound, profound is my courtyard, how profound?
Cloudy casement, foggy pavilion, tardy spring.
For whom is my flowery face withered?
Last night sweet was my dream,
Plum blossoms must have opened on the south branch.
How I regret the thin flowers and light branches!
Let not the barbarian flute pipe forth a mournful tune from the
    south pavilion.
Who knows that the rich perfume is gone?
Gentle wind, belated sun.
We are separated till the almond flowers bloom.

D. OTHER TOPICS

In the following rather ordinary poem, a quatrain devoted to hero worship, Li Ch'ing-chao writes about Hsiang Yü, the Emperor of Ch'u, who, after being defeated by the founder of the Han dynasty—Liu Pang, killed himself rather than return to the east side of the Wu River from whence he had come. Although this poem deals with a historical personage, the feeling expressed by Li Ch'ing-chao is somewhat different. Usually, Chinese poets have a strong sense of history; but, in writing about a historical character, they tend to express the same kind of feeling in the same kind of technique. Generally, they contrast the rise and fall of empires with the permanent features of nature; and they show the vanity of human effort by comparing the glory of the past to the ruin of today. They also sigh over battles fought long ago or weep over the "snows of yesteryear." Poems expressing such feelings are generally labeled "poems evoking antiquity." But in the sentiment expressed by Li Ch'ing-chao in her quatrain there is a departure from this type of Chinese poetry; she suggests that it is more honorable to die heroically than to live in humiliation. From this quatrain, one might infer that Li Ch'ing-chao was an ambitious woman:

Hsiang Yü

Living, one should be an outstanding man,
Dead, one should be an outstanding ghost.
Even today I forget not Hsiang Yü,
Who refused to go the east side of the river.

In the following poem, Li Ch'ing-chao fuses an external scene
with an internal emotion. It is late spring, and she has just awakened from a dream. What kind of dream did she have? A pleasant
one? A sad one? These questions are left unanswered. In this
poem—characterized by simplicity of language and by a highly
suggestive power—the melancholy aroused by the end of spring
is not really expressed but is suggested by the external scene. In
the poem, the passage of time, the changing of seasons evocative
of ephemeral youth are suggested by the faded plum blossoms
and by the grass that has grown tall enough to be used in the traditional folk game, "weeds." This game, formerly a favorite one of
the historical beauty Hsi Shih and her imperial lover, Emperor
Fu Ch'a of Wu, is played by two people, each of whom selects a
strong blade of grass; each then ties a knot at the end of the grass
stem; the two blades are interlocked at the knotted ends; and the
players pull the blades to see which one breaks first.

Modeled on *Washing Brook Sand*

Calm spring, Cold Food Festival,
A whiff of dying smoke of sandalwood hovering over the jade
    burner.
Awakening from a dream, I find my temple ornament under
    the hill-shaped pillow.
Swallows have not yet arrived, though people are playing the
    game of weeds.
Plum blossoms are over and catkins have appeared on the
    willows;
At dusk, a drizzling rain soaks my swing.

CHAPTER 4

Characteristics and Values

I *The Exceptional Chance*

IN THE preceding chapters, we have studied comprehensively the personality of Li Ch'ing-chao. We have examined the nature of her poetic works; we have applied systematically the method of analysis to imagery, symbols, allusions, suggestions, and other poetic devices in her *tz̆'u;* and we have assembled criticisms about her. It is now time to try to effect a synthesis of her personality and poetic experience; to this, I shall contribute ideas of my own.

In China, though poets have been as plentiful as spring flowers, poetesses have been as few as winter blossoms because of the subordinate position imposed upon women. In ancient times, Chinese ladies were condemned to live in the inner apartments, with embroidery and needlework as their chief occupations. When they had to go out to pay visits, they were borne by coolies in palanquins with curtains hermetically drawn. They were supposed to refrain from speaking aloud, expressing themselves, or planning their own future. They lived not like human beings but rather as inanimate objects, dependent and passive. It was Li Ch'ing-chao's good fortune to be born into a family where even her mother was highly cultured. From childhood Li Ch'ing-chao received a good education, and signs of genius were seen in her. She learned under favorable circumstances to read, write, paint, and play musical instruments. In a word, she was given the chance to develop her talents as well as her personality.

She also had the good fortune to be married to Chao Ming-ch'eng, a man who loved her dearly and who respected her genius. Not only did he admire her for her talents but he was also very liberal towards her, allowing her to live according to her fancy. She was free to drink, to write, to roam about the countryside, to sail on rivers and lakes, and to neglect cuisine and embroidery. This profound love and perfect understanding between the spouses were most beneficial to the blooming of Li Ch'ing-chao's genius. Compared to her feminine contemporaries, she was really an unproclaimed rebel.

II   *The Eternal Woman*

Yet the mental freedom and the revolt against the traditions of millennia did not mar Li Ch'ing-chao's femininity. In spite of her genius, erudition, and independence, she remained a woman, elegant and coquettish, tender and loving. She was conscious of her body: she wrote about her skin, delicate, smooth as jade and white as snow; about her slender waist; about her rippling eyes, flower-like face, cherry lips, small hands and perfumed cheeks. She likened her graceful movements to a trail of blue cloud. She was voluptuous, and she assumed esthetically the position of the eternal woman. She attached great importance to her appearance, and she loved dresses and jewelry. She used rouge and powder, adorned her coiffure with plum blossoms, and resorted to other artifices to enhance her charms.

In short, she was the embodiment of femininity. It was the eternal woman who made her elegant and coquettish, tender and affectionate. It was the eternal woman who made her amorous and languid, sensitive, and melancholy. It was the eternal woman who whispered: "Tonight, the muslin bed curtains, the pillows and the mat will be cool." It was the eternal woman who stuck flowers in her hair so that Chao Ming-ch'eng might compare them with her. It was the eternal woman who invited Chao Ming-ch'eng to renew the affairs of love when the moon cast its rays upon the flowers. It was the eternal woman who wrote: "Hardly have I turned my rippling eyes than he divines my thoughts." She was the eternal woman because she accepted gladly her body and her sex.

III   *The Temperament of Li Ch'ing-chao*

A good knowledge of Li Ch'ing-chao's family background and a careful study of her complete works show us that, temperamentally, she was aristocratic, romantic, sensual, supersensitive, passionate in love, and lukewarm in religion.

As we have already remarked, none of Li Ch'ing-chao's poems deal with warfare, agriculture, social injustice, or misgovernment. The absence of these subjects, which appear so often in other poets' works, can be explained by her family background. She came from an aristocratic family and was married into a aristocratic family. Though neither family was really rich, she never suffered privation, even in exile. This is proved by the fact that, when she was taking refuge in Chekiang, she was able to offer a high price to get back the books stolen from her. As her scope of interest lay in music, painting, and poetry, she naturally did not occupy herself with the toil of the peasants or the labor of the weavers. She was by nature and birth aristocratic, and her thoughts fully represented the class to which she belonged.

Li Ch'ing-chao was above all a sensualist in the extensive sense of the word. She loved to drink, and she wrote prolifically about wine. She liked fragrant odors and used beautiful words in praise of various kinds of incense and incense burners. She particularly liked certain flowers rich in perfume, such as the cassia flower and the plum blossom. She loved natural scenery and found much delight in the contemplation of the beauteous earth. She liked lovely sounds: she sang skilfully, as mentioned in one of her poems; and she played various musical instruments: the *sheng* and the lute. She was also sensitive to the joyous or mournful songs of birds.

Being a sensualist, she could not help being supersensitive. A fallen petal moved her to tears; the mournful sound of the cuckoo brought forth a multitude of sad images; a sip of wine rendered her languid; a cool evening inspired voluptuousness. She was sensitive to every aspect of the material world. Sight, odor, sound, color, and passion formed the essence of her poetry.

Throughout her writings, Li Ch'ing-chao mentioned "sky" but only twice in the religious sense of the word: once, when she wrote about a dream; once, when she said that it was Heaven that wanted the chrysanthemums to fade. In ancient China, there were two religions: Taoism and Buddhism. The former preached a detached attitude toward life, which it considered nothing but vanity; the latter, the extinction of desire and life. But Li Ch'ing-chao was indifferent to religion. She loved life and reality, upon which were built her intellectual activities. She never tried to find solace in religion when she was in despair. She never wrote about that spiritual communion between oneself and nature as preached by the Taoist. She described the beauties of nature, expressed joy or sorrow over them; but she never attained a selfless contemplation of it. She simply did not care for religion, because she loved the material world. She loved the beauties of nature, but nature seemed to assume no deeper significance in her eyes.

IV *Woman and Poetess Combined*

As we have already seen, Li Ch'ing-chao did not concern herself with social-mindedness, Confucian morality, Taoist mysticism, or Buddhist nihilism. She felt that the only vocation of
woman was love; this she attained. She loved tenderly and deeply,
and she wrote abundantly about her love. If poetry has been defined by the Chinese as "emotion expressed in language," then Li
Ch'ing-chao's poetry is truthful emotion expressed in beautiful
language. Although her unique collection of poems contains only
some fifty pieces of *tz'u,* and although the principal theme is love,
sincerity of emotion and richness of language make up for lack of
quantity and for monotony of subject. Li Ch'ing-chao's poetry
seems to be a monologue on love. This fact is exceptional; before
her time women seemed to have been largely mute on this subject, though men spoke effusively about it. She wrote naturally
and freely about love because she was really in love and was
proud of her femininity. She was sincere because she wrote according to what was in her heart. If she had tried to imitate men
and to depend more on intellect, her poems would have become
artificial and affected.

As I have already pointed out, Li Ch'ing-chao refused to be just
a passive woman devoted to serving men. She took the initiative
of expressing herself, of unveiling the quivering feminine soul.
Nevertheless, the stress she laid on love and femininity did not
lead her to excesses. She knew how to control the unburdening of
her heart and how to restrain her inspiration so that she could express herself with modesty and discretion. Her poems are confes-
sions but not entirely undisguised ones. Different parts of her
body, such as her rippling eyes, perfumed cheeks, and vermilion
lips, appear in her poems; but she does not go into detail such as
employed by Baudelaire in painting his Jeanne Duval. She suggests to Chao Ming-ch'eng: "Tonight, the muslin bed curtains,
pillows and mat will be cool," but she abstains from describing
the act of love, as Louise Labé does in her sonnets. Li Ch'ing-chao
is passionate without being licentious, real without being realistic,
voluptuous without being erotic.

An active existence is the source of literary inspiration. Many
writers lead a sterile life; consequently, every piece of their writing is more or less alike. Although a lady of the inner apartments,
Li Ch'ing-chao had rich experiences in life. She loved deeply; she

lived fully and intensely. She traveled far and wide. She was acquainted with various aspects of life. She knew the bliss of love, the sadness of parting, the yearning for the loved one, and the felicity of reunion. Her life was finally made unhappy by the premature death of an adored husband. In her old age, she was condemned to solitude and exile. The seeds of joy and sorrow sown on the spiritual soil bore a unique flower, the flower of love.

There is a virtual unity of theme in Li Ch'ing-chao's poetry, but it may be divided into three parts: poems of love, of separation, and of widowhood. Poems of love are compositions professing affection for her husband and are characterized by elegance of expression and tenderness of heart. Poems of separation, those written during Chao Ming-ch'eng's absence, are pathetic but illuminated with hope. And her poems of widowhood always glow with genius but are sustained on a heart-rending chord.

V *The Love Poems of Li Ch'ing-chao*

Although Li Ch'ing-chao's marriage was arranged by her parents as was customary in ancient China, she did feel true love for Chao Ming-ch'eng; that is why love is nearly the sole theme of her poetry. She sang of love in its manifold aspects: the bliss of married life, the sadness of parting, the yearning for the beloved, the ecstasy of reunion and the final despair of bereavement.

There are three things distinctive about Li Ch'ing-chao's love poems that I should like to point out. First, she does not sing of the object of love as most poets do. Second, she does not sing of love as an abstraction, nor exalt love as something absolute. Third, her love poems are presented in the form of esthetic or sensual emotion, but not as an outward sign of spiritual union.

As I have already mentioned, Li Ch'ing-chao was egocentric. She liked to be the center of her writings. Just as nature served as a frame for her own portrait, love was also a pretext for exalting herself. When E. E. Cummings sings of his love, he says:

> thy head is a quick forest
>   filled with sleeping birds
> thy breasts are swarms of white bees
>   upon the bough of thy body
> the body to me is April
> in whose armpits is the approach of spring

When Li Ch'ing-chao sings of her love, this is what she says:

> Lest my beloved one should say:
> Thy face is less fair than the flowers,
> I stuck them athwart in my hair
> So that he could compare.

In Li Ch'ing-chao's love poems, love is not sung of in the abstract sense of the word, or exalted as something absolute. She does not write as Ezra Pound in "An Immortality":

> Sing we for love and idleness,
> Naught else is worth the having.
>
> Though I have been in many a land,
> There is naught else in living.
>
> And I would rather have my sweet
> Though rose leaves die of grieving,
>
> Than do high deeds in Hungary
> To pass all men's believing.

But she does present love in the form of esthetic or sensual descriptions:

Hardly have I turned my rippling eyes
Than he divines my thoughts.

Through the red silk of my robe
Appears my skin, delicate, smooth, white as jade.
Smiling, I whisper to my beloved:
Tonight, the muslin bed curtains, the pillows and the mat will
   be cool.

She presents love also in the form of emotional expression:

> Things remain, he is no longer here, all is finished.
> Fain would I speak
> But tears precede my words.

In summary, her love poems are now serious, now lighthearted, now tender, now voluptuous, but never platonic.

VI *The Poetic Experience of Li Ch'ing-chao*

As I have already pointed out, Li Ch'ing-chao does not ex-pound any theory or philosophy of art. We cannot say that she wrote because art is a means of securing a temporary escape from the imperfections of life, or because it offers the possibility of rising permanently above them. Nor can we say that she wrote because art made her realize the illusory nature of the empirical world and the reality of the higher and non-attached spirit within us. On the contrary, I would venture to say that Li Ch'ing-chao's poetry is the culmination of a successful existence. She enjoyed the indoors and outdoors; she even enjoyed the idleness of the sickbed. She lived life fully, and she undertook the task of pro-claiming the glory of all that exists. She wrote for her own pleas-ure; she wrote according to her feelings and moods. She counted on poetic experience to enrich the world and her ego more fully than she might through normal experience. To her, art was a clarification of world-consciousness and self-consciousness. She identified truth and beauty, and combined poetry with reality. Her voice was never harsh or scornful, but beautiful and touch-ing.

Unlike many modern writers who paint reality as absurd or de-grading, she found delight in reality. She did not ignore sorrow-ful aspects of life such as separation, old age, and death; but she beautified the bright as well as the dark side of life, accepting the negative aspects of existence as inevitable, and taking them philo-sophically and poetically. When one looks at the world in a fully esthetic way, good and evil, joy and pain, peace and anxiety be-come different parts of a universal symphony, or various elements of a sublime spectacle. As we see in *Hamlet*, the drowning of Ophelia is endowed with a pathetic beauty, so we see through the mirror of the poetry of Li Ch'ing-chao reality made sublime.

VII *The World in the Poetry of Li Ch'ing-chao*

When commenting on poetry, Chinese critics never fail to talk about *chin-chieh*, which I translate as "world." A poem is con-sidered superb when the world in it is lofty and remote. In my opinion, this lofty and remote world in Chinese poetry corre-sponds to what is called the "unknown" sought after by mod-ern Western poets. It means that unfamiliar world explored or created by the poet to which we cannot attain through normal experience. A poet does not merely narrate an experience, take it as the content of his poem, and fix it into a pattern. On the contrary, he is prompted by a past experience—a sentiment, a thought, or an event—to write. When he searches for the right words, the right sounds, and the right images, the original experience is transmuted into something new and unknown; and a poetic world is created. This is what Henri Michaux means when he says: "I write in order that what was true should no longer be true."

In the broad sense of the word, the world in poetry is a fusion of the external and internal aspects of life: the former includes not only natural scenery but also events and actions; the latter, not only emotion but also thought, memory, vision, and sensation. In other words, the world in poetry is the reflection of the poet's external environment and the expression of his inner consciousness. Each poem has a world of its own. A world described as lofty and remote is the most appreciated in Chinese poetry. In this regard, Henri Michaux makes another remark that deserves a passing notice. He says that it is not necessary for a poet to have more than one major sentiment, but that one and only one will suffice, be it love, hatred, envy, or revolt. If a poet has one basic sentiment, he will be able to build upon it a universe of his own. As Li Ch'ing-chao's major sentiment is love, the world in her poetry is narrower than the definition given in the preceding paragraph and is limited to a fusion of emotion and scene. For the most part, her poetry involves expressing internal emotion and describing external scene. But sometimes it is hard to separate one from the other, since Chinese poetry is rich in suggestion and association. For instance, the following lines contain only external scenes:

> I mount the high pavilion.
> Mountains in disorder, vast countryside, thin mist,
> Thin mist.
> After the crows returned homeward to perch,
> Horns are heard in the evening air.

Yet how effectively do they convey the feeling of desolation and solitude, just as the "Preludes" of T. S. Eliot, though consisting of only external scenes, conveys the feeling of boredom and depression:

> The winter evening settles down
> With smell of steaks in passageways.
> Six o'clock.
> The burnt-out ends of smoky days.
> And now a gusty shower wraps
> The grimy scraps
> Of withered leaves about your feet
> And newspapers from vacant lots;
> The showers beat
> On broken blinds and chimney-pots,
> And at the corner of the street
> A lonely cab-horse steams and stamps.
> And then the lighting of the lamps.

In order to create a world that is lofty and remote, Li Ch'ing-chao resorts above all to words. Not only does she explore the external and internal worlds but also the possibilities of language. She attaches great importance to words. She either tries to find proper words and sounds for new worlds of experiences, or new words for familiar worlds. The emotional world of love, separation, nostalgia, joy, and sorrow is as old as mankind itself; but Li Ch'ing-chao knows how to express it in different ways so as to create an unfamiliar world from familiar experiences.

By seeking images, symbols, analogies, and words charged with implication and association; by attempting to capture subtle shades of feeling and elusive moods, she reaches that lofty and remote poetic world. This world necessarily involves unusual ways of using language with new expressions, new combinations of sense and sound, new images, new symbols, and new analogies. Though Li Ch'ing-chao is without profound thought, her true emotion and her power of communication suffice to make her a great poet.

VIII *Imagery, Symbolism, and Analogy*

Ever since the dawn of history, Chinese poets have expressed their thoughts and feelings by images, symbols, and analogies instead of by expressing them in simple, direct language. As we consider the use of these devices in Chinese poetry from age to age, let us read the first stanza of the first poem of the first anthology, *The Book of Odes:*

> *Kuan, kuan,* two plovers sing to each other
> On an islet of the river.
> The quiet and ignored young lady
> Is the spouse of the Lord.

At first glance, there may seem to be no connection between the first two lines and the rest. But Chinese language in poetry is extremely concise and often dispenses with connecting particles. The image of the plovers is used to symbolize the harmony between Emperor Wen of the Chou dynasty and the queen, since the poem is written in praise of the virtue of the imperial spouses.

In *The Poems of Ch'u,* the second anthology of Chinese poetry, *Li Sao* is highly appreciated for its allusion and symbolism. Ch'ü Yüan, the author, was a loyal minister of King Huai of the Ch'u State of the feudal period. For a long time he enjoyed the full confidence of the king, but he was finally calumniated by jealous and vicious rivals. Fallen into disgrace with the king, he was condemned to exile. He then composed *Li Sao* to give free outlet to his woe. In this long poem, he used fragrant herbs and flowers as symbols of virtue and poisonous plants as those of vice: "In the morning I drink the dewdrops from the magnolia,/In the evening, I eat the fallen petals of the autumn chrysanthemum." Here the acts of drinking the dewdrops from the magnolia and of eating the fallen petals of the autumn chrysanthemum signify the cultivation of virtue.

As mentioned earlier, under the Eastern Han dynasty, Lady Pan Chieh-yü was for a long time the chief favorite of Emperor Ch'eng. When she was at last supplanted by a younger, more attractive rival, she presented the sovereign with a fan on which was inscribed her famous poem entitled *The Plaintive Song.* Because of its relevancy here, I shall repeat the poem:

> I tore off a piece of Shantung silk
> As white as frost and snow.
> I cut it to make a fan
> As round as the moon.
> It will be a close companion of thee.
> Its movement producing a gentle breeze.
> Often it fears the approach of autumn
> When cold wind will sweep away the dying summer's heat.

It will then be abandoned in a bamboo chest,
Losing your love and favor.

In this poem, the author does not compare her own disgrace directly to the abandoned fan at the arrival of autumn, but readers who know the sad story of the imperial concubine will not fail to see the suggested analogy. Moreover, the poem may also be regarded as the monologue of a fan expressing its fears and sorrows. Thus the allusion to the fan fulfills a dual function: it describes an immediate object, and it points to an analogy between the fan and the one whom it represents.

As the history of Chinese poetry developed, imagery, symbolism, and analogy came to be more frequently used. From the T'ang dynasty onward, Chinese poetry became replete with hackneyed images such as "cherry lips" and "flowery faces." Such clichés, though tolerated because consecrated by time-honored usage, reveal a lack of originality. By contrast, Li Ch'ing-chao is to be highly appreciated for her original images. For instance, we have these "Human voices are stilled. The bright moon shines athwart,/Soaking the pear flowers. . . ." In these lines, the verb "soaking" constitutes an original though indirect image because it suggests that the bright moon is to be compared to water.

It is quite common to compare a beautiful lady to flowers, but such verse as "my coverlet unfurls its red waves" is most original. The analogy between the undulations of the waves and the large folds of the red coverlet is precise and original. In Li Ch'ing-chao's poetry, the conventional comparison of beautiful flowers to girls has given rise to several interesting images:

When the west wind stirs the screen,
I am as frail as the yellow chrysanthemum.

Thin flowers loaded with heavy dewdrops,
Thin robe soaked with light perspiration.

Sometimes she modifies a time-honored image and derives a slightly different one from it. For instance, "windy hair" and "frost temples" are modified versions of the hackneyed image "cloudlike coiffure." *

* The reader should note, however, that the poetess used the expression "cloudlike coiffure" on one occasion (see page 89).

It is easy to liken one thing to another through imagery, but it is difficult to conceive precise and striking images such as:

> The melting gold of the sinking sun,
> The gathering jade of the evening clouds.

> A thousand skeins of sorrow bind my tender heart.

Imagery can serve the double purpose of describing external scenes and expressing internal emotions. In "The scent has vanished, the smoke is gone, the incense burner is chilled,/To accompany my heart cold as water," the sandalwood burned to ash and the chilled incense burner are conjured up by Li Ch'ing-chao to describe an immediate object, as well as to express her sorrow and bereavement.

In Chinese poetry, there are two kinds of symbols: the conventional and the personal. A conventional symbol is an object chosen by usage to represent something, such as the chrysanthemum for solitude and nobility of soul, the wild goose for the traveler, the willow branch for farewell. Personal symbols are individual inventions of the poet to create an atmosphere, and to represent a state of mind, an outlook of life, or his own personality. Since style is the man himself, the imagery that contributes to the style can provide a clue to character. Therefore, from the personal symbols used by Li Ch'ing-chao in her poetry, we discover the principal traits of her personality.

She is egocentric. For the most part, she herself is involved in the images:

> Graceful, slim, what can I be likened to?
> A trail of blue clouds.

> My perfumed, jadelike skin,
> As smooth as snow.

> When the west wind stirs the screen,
> I am as frail as the yellow chrysanthemum.

> Only my tears are left,
> As abundant as yellow plum rain.

She is coquettish; she likes to please men:

Opening my vermilion lips,
How skilfully I sing!
Every word is charm and coquetry.

Smiling, I draw aside the hibiscus-colored bed curtains,
My perfumed cheek against the precious incense stick.
Hardly have I turned my rippling eyes than he divines my
        thoughts.

Beholding a visitor's approach,
I rush away, bashful,
Wearing only stockings, gold hairpins slipping.
Yet back I turn at the door
And feign to smell the green plums.

Lest my beloved one should say:
Your face is less fair than the flowers,
I stuck them athwart in my cloudy hair
So that he could compare.

She is elegant:

> Under the candlelight
> Shines my phoenix hairpin.

> A gold bird flies on my cloudlike coiffure.

> Wearing emerald-adorned coiffure
> And gold-threaded, willowlike snow-white belts,
> We rivaled one another in elegance.

> Tears mingled with powder stain my silk robe.

She is a lady of leisure. And the word "leisure" does not mean
that state of mind free from worldly cares and desires, which we
often find in such philosophical verses as the following:

> A jade kettle with a purchase of spring.*
> A shower on the thatched hut
> Wherein sits a gentle scholar,

* Translation by Giles, *op. cit.*, p. 181.

> With bamboos growing right and left
> And white clouds in the newly clear sky,
> And birds flitting in the depth of trees.
> Then pillowed on his lute in the green shade,
> A waterfall tumbling overhead,
> Leaves dropping, not a word spoken,
> The man placid, like a chrysanthemum,
> Noting down the flowery glory of the season—
> A book worthy to be read.

In this poem, the poet has emptied his mind of worries or longing and has identified it with the objects surrounding him. From the bamboo to the clouds and birds, everything seems as tranquil as the poet himself. He is idle, but he enjoys his idleness. The season with all its glories will pass by, but the poet takes it philosophically and gives no sign of regret over it. He has raised "leisure" to the level of philosophic contemplation.

In the works of Li Ch'ing-chao, however, leisure rarely has such philosophical significance. It means either being unoccupied or is of that nonchalant, listless state of mind so reminiscent of Baudelaire's ennui. When she is at leisure, she may busy herself with make-up and attire:

> Under the shadows of plum blossoms,
> Fresh is my nocturnal make-up.

> When the empire was prosperous,
> We ladies were much at leisure
> And highly priced the fifteenth day of each moon.
> Wearing emerald-adorned coiffure
> And gold-threaded, willowlike, snow-white belts,
> We rivaled one another in elegance.

She may also contemplate external scenes without being able to free her mind of melancholy, depression, or longing:

> Only the flowing water in front of my pavilion
> Knows that my eyes are fixed thereupon.
> Where there are my strained eyes,
> There is a newborn sorrow.

Within the spring casement, haggard and worn by ennui,
I lean not against the balcony.

I fear that the small boat of the Double Stream
Could not bear so much sadness.

Deep, deep is my courtyard, how deep?
Cloudy casement, foggy pavilion, tardy spring.
For whom is my flowery face withered?

Wild geese pass by
And grieve my heart.

Alone I wait by the window,
How can the day get dark?

In the depth of my silent chamber,
A thousand skeins of sorrow bind my heart.

Let not the deep cup be filled with amber-colored wine,
Languor seizes me before drunkness.

Outside the idle casement, in the small courtyard, spring is
advanced.
Screens being unrolled, heavy are the shadows.
Speechless, I play on my jade lute.

Due to spring melancholy,
I am too weary to comb my hair.

The wind is calm, the soil is perfumed, the flowers are fallen.

The day is dying, I am too weary to comb my hair.

From these examples, we can say that leisure in Li Ch'ing-
chao's poetry is a sophisticated, emotional attitude, a subtle and
elusive mood slightly tinged with melancholy.

IX *Other Poetic Devices: Suggestion, Allusion, Antithesis, Derivation, and Reduplication*

For the most part, Li Ch'ing-chao uses simple, natural language in her poetry; but sometimes she also expresses herself in an oblique way by means of different poetic devices such as suggestion, allusion, antithesis, derivation, and repetition.

For instance, in the *tz'u* modeled on *Nostalgia of the Flute in the Phoenix Pavilion*, devoted to the theme of separation, she expresses her longing for Chao Ming-ch'eng by saying:

> Only the flowing water in front of my pavillion
> Knows that my eyes are fixed thereupon all day long.
> Where there are my strained eyes,
> There is a newborn sorrow.

In this poem, the poetess does not say directly that she pines for her husband; it is the flowing water in front of her pavilion that should know that her eyes are fixed upon it; it is as if she wanted the water to bear witness to her longing. Water is inanimate, but to the poet it is endowed with life and sentiment. If she had merely said that she pined for her husband, the poem would have been colorless, without flavor. In the same poem, she expresses her weariness with these lines: "Let the dust cover my precious coiffeuse,/And the sun climb up the hooks of my bed curtains." During the absence of Chao Ming-ch'eng, she dallies in her bed and is too weary to think of make-up. As poetic language is inclined to be concrete and picturesque, a coiffeuse covered with dust and the sun climbing up the hooks of her curtains more effectively suggest the mental and physical weariness of the author.

In a poem written in her old age and widowhood, she expresses the helplessness of her situation in the following way: "Heaps of yellow chrysanthemums upon the soil./Faded and spoiled,/Who cares to pluck them?" The unplucked and withered flowers are she, haggard and worn. Her beauty has faded like the flowers, and she is left alone in her old age. Nobody pities her, just as nobody is interested in faded flowers.

Ever since the T'ang dynasty, a great deal of Chinese poetry has been highly allusive. There are two views regarding allusion. The one condemns allusion as being pedantic and artificial, and as stripping poetry of its purity, freshness, and originality. The other opines that sometimes allusion is justified because it can be used to present a situation tersely; to draw an analogy between a past event and a present one; or to provide a contrast between them.

In a *tz'u* modeled on *Partridges in the Sky*, which concerns homesickness, Li Ch'ing-chao wrote: "Wang Chung-hsüan is still more grieved,/Thinking of his distant home." Wang Chung-hsüan, a well-known poet, lived at the end of the Eastern Han dynasty. It was a period of trouble; the poet had left his home town in order to take refuge in Chinchow. In his exile, he wrote a piece of rhymed prose devoted to nostalgia. By alluding to him, Li Ch'ing-chao suggests that she is also living in times of trouble, far away from home, and that she too can find her only solace in poetry. If she did not use an allusion but wrote directly "I am the more grieved, thinking of my distant home," she would appear to be indulging in self-pity and excessive sentimentality.

Allusion, when used occasionally, does no harm. When abused, it renders poetry lifeless: it makes a poem look like a list of phantoms. Nevertheless, Li Ch'ing-chao once effectively used eleven allusions in a poem about white chrysanthemums. Professor She Hsüeh-man wrote in this regard: "Li Ch'ing-chao's poetic language is as simple and plain as colloquial speech. Yet, when she uses allusion, it is natural and full of grace." If she had not used eleven allusions to describe the beauty, perfume, and qualities of white chrysanthemums, she would have overused the adjectives without being able to present that flower as she wished.

As I have already mentioned, allusion, instead of drawing an analogy, can also provide a contrast between a past event and a present situation. In a *tz'u*—written while separated from her husband and entitled *Hsing Hsiang Tzu*—she alludes to the legend about the annual reunion of the mythical Spinning Maid and the Cowherd. In that poem, instead of drawing an analogy between the heavenly couple and her own situation, she contrasts her indefinite separation from her husband with the happy annual meeting of the divine spouses.

Whether allusion serves to draw an analogy or provide a contrast between a story of the past and a present experience, it enhances poetic effect. Moreover, by evoking a chain of associations with the past, it can extend the significance of the present context because an event or a person alluded to has a broader significance than does a single epithet. For instance, to describe the scent of white chrysanthemums, the poet can merely overuse adjectives like "fragrant," "odorous," "aromatic," "sweet," and so on. When Li Ch'ing-chao compares the odor of that flower to the perfume stolen by Han Shou, she endows her poem with additional implication.

In China, poets are allowed to borrow the original writings of previous or contemporary poets and to twist them slightly so as to derive new expressions. When Chao Ming-ch'eng was leaving for Tunglai where he had been appointed magistrate, Li Ch'ing-chao addressed a farewell poem to him; the last verse read: "By luck, I can count on wild geese to send my letters;/Tunglai is less far than P'englai." In this verse, the idea of sending letters by wild geese to Tunglai is derived from the following poem by Li Shang-yin, a famous T'ang poet whose writings were rich in allusion and personal symbolism. Li Shang-yin was said to have been involved in a secret love affair with a Taoist nun. To avoid scandal, he often wrote untitled poems.

Hard it is for us to meet and hard to part.
Powerless is the east wind, all the flowers are faded and gone.
The spring silkworm will end its thread only when dying,
The candle will dry its tears only when burnt to ash.
In the morning, facing the mirror, she fears that her cloudy hair
    will turn gray,
At night, she must feel that the moon is cold.
P'englai lies at no great distance from here,
May the Bluebird eagerly convey to her my tender thoughts.

In Chinese, the word "hard" has two different meanings: "difficult" and "unbearable." In the first line, the word "hard" carries at the same time these two meanings. This poem is an expression of the poet's love for the nun who lives nearby but with whom he cannot openly communicate. Therefore, he begins the poem by saying not only that it is difficult for them to see each other, but also that they find it unbearable to leave each other when the sad hour of parting comes. The second line apparently describes the dying spring, but in fact the poet likens himself to the east wind and his ladylove to the flowers. The east wind is powerless to prevent the flowers from dying, just as he is powerless to prevent her youth from fading away. In the third and fourth lines, more personal images are introduced: just as the silkworm imprisons itself in the cocoon woven by its own silk, so does the poet wrap himself in woeful thoughts. Just as the candle is burned to ash by its own fire, so does the poet consume himself by the flame of his unfulfilled passion.

In the next couplet, the poet imagines his beloved sitting in the morning in front of her mirror, fearing the passing away of her youth; and he imagines her as lingering on during the night and feeling lonely in the cold moonlight. In the next-to-last line, P'englai, a dwelling of Taoist immortals, is a symbol of bliss. Where the loved one is, there bliss is. The Bluebird of the last line is a divine messenger. As the abode of the lady is compared to P'englai, only a divine messenger can send her messages.

In her farewell poem to Chao Ming- ch'eng, Li Ch'ing-chao, borrowing Li Shang-yin's allusion to P'englai and the Bluebird, suggests that, if the Bluebird can be sent as a messenger to the distant fairyland of P'englai, she will be able to communicate much more easily with her husband by sending a wild goose as a messenger.

In a *tzŭ* modeled on *The Fisherman's Pride,* which recorded a dream of hers, Li Ch'ing-chao wrote: "On wind-back, the roc-bird is setting out for a ninety-thousand-mile journey." This line is derived from Chuang Tzu, the early Taoist philosopher who wrote: "The enormous roc-bird rides on the wind for a ninety-thousand-mile journey. Its wings are like clouds hanging in the sky."

There is a natural tendency in Chinese towards antithesis. For instance, instead of asking: "What is the height?" one asks: "What is the high-low?" Instead of asking: "What is the size?" one asks: "What is the big-small?" Instead of saying "everywhere," one says "in the big streets and the small lanes." In describing the crowd on a festival day, one says "men in red and women in green." This inclination towards poetic antithesis can be explained by the fact that monosyllabic characters lend themselves easily to antithesis, for each of the antithetical couplets must contain the same number of syllables, be they monosyllabic, dissyllabic, or of more than two syllables.

If we try to define antithesis or the antithetical couplet, we can say that it consists in constructing two lines in such a way that the characters in each line are identical in number and that they respond to each other in ideas, tones, and grammar. Ideas may be analogous or opposed. Flat tones should respond to sharp tones. The grammatical role of each character or term should be the same. We cite the following examples: a five-syllabic antithetical couplet: "The bright moon shines among the pines,/"The pure fountain flows on the rocks"; "Green, green grows the grass by the river,/Thick, thick stands the willow in the garden." Or a seven-syllabic antithetical couplet by Li Ch'ing-chao, wherein the ideas are opposed: "The new shoots have already grown into bamboo beneath the perrons,/The fallen petals have all gone into the nests of the swallows."

From these examples, we can see that antithetical couplets, whether identical or opposed in idea, enhance poetic effect. In the first example, the two lines extracted from a poem by the T'ang poet Wang Wei are identical in meaning and serve to depict the night scenes of an autumn evening in the mountains. In the second, the two lines are also identical in meaning and serve to describe the luxuriance of spring vegetation. In the last example, the two lines, though serving the same purpose of describing the passing away of spring, are opposed in idea. In the first line, the new shoots have grown and become bamboo; in the last, the flowers have fallen and mingled with mud, and are used by the swallows to fortify their nests. Although both lines describe the same thing, there is a contrast between the luxuriance of the bamboo and the withering of the flowers.

Just as there is a natural inclination in Chinese towards antithesis, there is also a tendency towards repetition. In daily conversation, a word is repeated to stress an idea. For instance, when accompanying a visitor to the door, we say, "Walk slowly, slowly" (*Man man tsou*) to suggest that he should be careful all along the road. When seeing a child off to school, we recommend, "Study well, well" (*Hao hao nien shu*), to insist that he work hard. Other examples such as "green, green," "sweet, sweet;" "small, small;" and "far, far" are common in colloquial speech. In poetry, a monosyllabic character or a polysyllabic expression is often seen repeated. The former is called "repeated words" (*tieh tzu*) and the latter is "repeated sentences" (*tieh chü*).

Generally speaking, two kinds of repetition are distinguished in poetry. First, there are words repeated for emphasis, such as *chiao chiao* (bright, bright), *ch'i ch'i* (sad, sad), *mien mien* (endless, endless), and *yü yü* (luxuriant, luxuriant). Second there are monosyllabic words repeated to form new compounds with independent meaning, such as *yeh yeh* (night after night), and *nien nien* (year after year). Sometimes by putting a compound formed by either of the repetitions mentioned above before an expression beginning with the same word that forms the compound, the poet produces something strikingly original. For instance, in describing a young bird that has lost its mother, Po Chü-i, the popular T'ang poet, wrote: "*Yeh-yeh-yeh-pan t'i*" (Night after night, at midnight, it cries). The word "yeh" is repeated three times so as to form a triplication, but in fact the third *yeh* should go with the word *pan* (half) to mean "midnight."

As Li Ch'ing-chao was a great phonetician, she explored extensively the musical effects of language in poetry and often resorted to duplication or triplication. The duplications used by Li Ch'ing-chao are of various kinds, so as to produce different auditory effects. Some are those used to show coquetry and femininity: "Descending from the swing,/Languorously I trim my tiny, tiny hands."

Certain reduplications are used to create atmosphere:

> Silent, silent is the world,
>
> Fair, fair is the moon.
>
> The screens being unrolled,
> Heavy, heavy are the shadows.

Others are used to stress feelings of sadness and weariness:

> Gray, gray turns my hair.
>
> Endless, endless is my regret.
>
> Year after year (*nien nien*), in front of my mirror,
> Listlessly, I adorn my coiffure with plum flowers.

Still others are used as onomatopeia:

> Dripping, dripping, fine rain is heard in the silent inn.
>
> At dusk, the fine rain on the plane tree
> Falls with a pitter-patter, a pitter-patter.

Not only does she use reduplication, but triplication is also found in her works. In describing her courtyard, she writes: *"T'ing yüan shen shen shen chi hsü?"* (Courtyard, deep, deep, deep to what extent?). Properly translated, the verse should read: Deep, deep is my courtyard, how deep? As the order of words in a Chinese sentence often differs from English, the word "deep" repeated three times forms a triplication in Chinese but not in English.

Not only does Li Ch'ing-chao resort to duplication and triplication, but she also repeats sentences:

> In front of my window, I planted banana trees,
> Their shadows fill up my courtyard,
> Their shadows fill up my courtyard.
>
> Sad is the midnight rain upon my pillow.
> Every drop is sadness,
> Every drop is sadness.

From the repetition found in Li Ch'ing-chao's works, be it repeated words or sentences, we can see that not only is it pleasant to the ear but that it also serves to stress ideas and to create an atmosphere or a state of mind. Consequently, it is a very effective poetic device.

X *An Evaluation*

Poetry has been defined by Chinese critics in many ways. Confucius stated: "If you do not study poetry, you will not know how to talk. If you do not study poetry, you will not know how to live. Poetry serves to inspire emotion, to help observation, to make you fit for company, to express grievances, to teach you how to serve your father at home and the prince abroad, to enable you learn the correct names of many birds, beasts, herbs and trees." Tzu Hsia (a disciple of Confucius) saw these values; "Nothing approaches *The Book of Odes* in setting up standards of right and wrong, in moving heaven and earth and in appealing to spirits and divinities. The ancient kings used it to perpetuate the tie between husband and wife, to perfect filial reverence, to deepen the human relationship, to beautify moral instruction and to improve the customs of the people." Or, in the opinion of K'ung Ying-ta (a T'ang literary critic), "Poetry encourages the good and condemns the evil." And Wang Kuo-wei (a famous contemporary literary critic) thought "A poet should be at once inside and outside the universe and life; inside in order to describe, outside in order to observe."

According to the philosophical school, poetry should reflect Nature and resemble it in its impenetrable, impassible character. Poetry is neither moral teaching nor self-expression; it is an embodiment of the poet's vision of the world. Although Li Ch'ing-chao did not expound theories of art to tell us what poetry is, or should be, or how it should be written, yet we can say with certainty that for her poetry is not moral instruction or that contemplative state of mind preached by Taoist and Buddhist philosophical schools. But, according to the individualist school, poetry is the expression of one's heart. In writing poetry, one must express what is sincerely felt in the heart and what is felt at heart in common with others. Because of this concept, every word is like a teardrop. And because poetry expresses common heartfelt feelings, it inspires readers to shed tears in response. Consequently, if one wants to be a real poet, one must have genuine emotion. Li Ch'ing-chao is a pure lyric poet—personal, esthetic, subjective, emotional. Her poetry is the reflection of her personality, feelings, and life.

Her language is colorful, elegant, and musical. The way she expresses herself is subtle, but she is not more concerned with elegance of style as are those who regard poetry as a pure literary exercise and manifestation of erudition and culture than with sentiment. She writes when she really has something to say; she does not write merely for the sake of writing, like those men of letters who consider poetry an elegant pastime and meet regularly to compose poems on given subjects, and echo each other's poems by using the same rhyme. When Li Ch'ing-chao has something to say, she then concerns herself with how to say it.

From her short essay on *tz'u*, we can see that she attaches the same importance to language, music, scenes, and emotions. She is perfectly right—emotion alone will not make us poets; neither will scene, music, and language. Emotion is the essence or substance of poetry, but one must have adequate language with which to express it in order to establish harmony between the theme and the style; for we cannot say that a baby's crying or an angry woman's shouting is poetry. Good poetry is like good wine: it must be well-distilled to leave out the sediment. Emotions are like grapes; they must be pressed and distilled in order to produce pure wine. Just as a wine producer must have a wine press and a distillery for the grapes, a poet must have adequate language for the emotions. Without adequate language, a poet cannot discriminate, for emotion in its original state is not poetry: it is sheer bathos and declamation. That is why Wordsworth defines poetry as the "impassioned expression of emotion."

Others may consider Li Ch'ing-chao frivolous and shallow, and advocate that poetry should exercise a moral influence. But unfortunately, serious poetry—be it political, social, or moral—carries in itself a perishable element. Nothing is so perishable as propagandist literature; for, once the problem that is the object of attack is solved, the poem that attacks it loses its *raison d'être*. For this reason, Shakespeare is more durable than Ibsen; now that women are liberated, *A Doll's House* has less impact, while *Othello* retains its contemporary character because jealousy is a sentiment that will last as long as mankind itself. Moreover, satire, however poetic it may be, is not universal in character. If it is directed against the rich, it will find its way only into the hearts of the poor; if it is directed against one political party, it will be appreciated only by its enemies. If it is directed against the government, it can find an echo only in the hearts of the people. Emotion is universal and eternal in man; in poetry, only that which is lyrical is assured of universality and immortality. If emotion expressed in a poem is sincere, readers will be moved to tears, no matter who they are, how they are, or what they are.

After having translated and examined nearly all of Li Ch'ing-chao's poems and applied the critical-analytical method to them, I am able to state without hesitation that the universality and immortality of her poetry lies in the sincerity of her emotion and in the elegance of her expression. Others, however, have also praised her. For example, She Mei-Sou wrote that she had sincerity and that "from the Ming dynasty onward, sentimentalists have admired her for her tenderness and delicacy; visionaries have admired her for her imagination."

And Miao Yüeh wrote: "There are three things about Li Ch'ing-chao which I would like to point out: first, she is a pure *tz'u* writer. *Tz'u* originated from poetry, but differs from it not only in form but also in essence. What poetry expresses is already sentiment, but poetry is insufficient to express certain sentiments which are even more subtle, more delicate, more elusive and more vague, and a new form of expression is required. That is how *tz'u* has come into being. Of course, not everyone is possessed of this kind of subtle and elusive sentiment, and only those who possess it are born *tz'u* writers. Under the Sung, there were many born *tz'u* writers such as Yen Chi-tao, Ch'in Kuan, Chou Pang-yen, Chiang K'uei and Li Ch'ing-chao. As the latter was a woman, her sensitivity is still greater and richer than that of men of letters of her time. Endowed with a profound sensibility and a natural gift for poetry, she utters naturally what is sincerely felt in her heart.

"Second, the world she creates in her *tz'u* is lofty and transcendental. First-rank poets often have lofty ideals and are free from any kind of restraint. They are emotional without being enthralled by emotion; they are lovers of beauteous objects without being enslaved by objects; their thoughts, though real and profound, carry with them a certain airiness. The poetic world created by Li Ch'ing-chao is elevated and pure. When you read her *tz'u*, you feel as though you were in front of a wonderful landscape, where you see not only mountains and rivers, but also white clouds forever drifting in a clear, blue autumn sky.

"Third, Li Ch'ing-chao is an original and independent *tz'u* writer. She relies more upon spontaneous feeling than on technique, erudition or imitation. If one of her *tz'u* happens to bear a great likeness to that of a previous poet, it is only because she feels and expresses herself in a similar way. Only mediocre poets seek to imitate; imitation rarely produces resemblance in spirit. Li Ch'ing-chao's poetry combines the moderation of Yen Shu, the profundity of Ou-yang Hsiu, the grace of Chang Hsien, the sensibility of Liu Yung, the freedom of Su Shih, the melancholy of Ch'in Kuan, the sublimity of Yen Chi-tao, and the elegance of Hu Chü. Generally speaking, her *tz'u* is fresh and pure, graceful and free, characterized by sensibility and delicacy during her early period, and by profundity and power during her old age."

But the poetry of Li Ch'ing-chao is more than sensitivity and emotional reaction; for what makes poetry is in part its musical effect—the effect of language that makes it agreeable to the ear. Li Ch'ing-chao in her essay on *tz'u* blames Yen Yüan-hsien, On-yang Hsiu, and Su Tz-chan for ignoring phonetics; Yen Shu-yüan for lacking description; Ho Fang-huei for lacking subtance; and Ch'in Shao-yu for not being sober enough in language though rich in emotion. Although emotion and scene are called by two different names, in Chinese poetry they are inseparable. One is

rarely mentioned without the other, for one can suggest or reveal
the other. A poem that seeks to convey emotion without description can rarely attain sublime simplicity and sobriety. A poem
consisting only of descriptions of scenes cannot be considered
genuine poetry.

As for Li Ch'ing-chao's poetry, it is minute in description, elegant and colorful in style, and pleasant to the ear. If she seeks
to convey emotion without description, she is simple, natural, and
sober; and these qualities are to be noted in the following lines,
which contain a superficial description of evening scenes, but
which also still suggest impressively the feeling of sadness and
desolation:

> Who sits by the lit window?
> We two: my shadow and I.
> At bedtime when the lamp wick is burned out,
> Even my shadow abandons me.
> What to do? What to do?
> Poor me!

Even when she writes descriptive poetry, she manages to convey
her personal feelings through the suggestiveness of imagery:

> I mount the high pavilion.
> Mountains in disorder, vast plain, thin mist,
> Thin mist.
> After the crows returned homeward to perch,
> Horns are heard in the evening air.

In other sections of this book I have also illustrated by example
how Li Ch'ing-chao explored the musical effects of language by
using reduplication and triplication—a device much admired by
Change Kuei-i, the Sung critic, who wrote: "The repetition of
words in the *tz'u* modelled on *Andante* is comparable to the skill-
fulness of the Lady Kung Sun, the famous sword dancer of the
T'ang dynasty. The fourteen repeated words in the first three
verses in *Andante* may be likened to large and small pearls dropping into a jade plate. Talented men of letters are not wanting
in this dynasty, but none of them has ever employed fourteen
reduplicated words in one poem."

In summary, Li Ch'ing-chao is to be appreciated neither for

her variety of inspiration nor for her profundity of thinking. Her poetry contains no philsophical or religious ideas, it preaches no way of thinking or attitude towards life. She is a pure lyric poet, subjective and emotional. Nevertheless, emotion, once expressed in her works, ceases to be particular to herself. No matter how paradoxical it may seem, there is this miracle about great works of art: though individual artists seek their own language to express their own feelings, their success is never individual in character. It is the eternal or universal man who seeks expression. We find universality in their creation of art, in their discovery of "truth," in their expression of emotion. Li Ch'ing-chao uses her own language to express her own emotion, but the emotion expressed in her poetry is such that it causes a spiritual flow of ourselves into her poetic world and esthetic vision. The poetic world in Li Ch'ing-chao's works is a fusion of emotion and scene; and this poetic world is so real that it transports us into it, enables us to see certain things and feel certain emotions imaginatively, and allows us to experience a state of being that we may not have in real life.

The great literary critic, the late Dr. Hu Shih, said that we should not moan without being sick. It seems to me that what is most precious in the works of Li Ch'ing-chao is the sincerity of joy or despair and the expression of sentiment that stems from the depth of her heart. We human beings, with our ups and downs, joys and pains, hopes and fears, discover in Li Ch'ing-chao not only an individual poet but also a great creator who, through her own experience, speaks for us all a language that is universal and eternal.

Selected Bibliography

PRIMARY SOURCES

Shu Yü Tz'u. Kaoshiung: The Ta Chung Book Company, 1964. A collection of fifty tz'u by Li Ch'ing-chao.

Chin Shih Lu Hou Hsü. Kaoshiung: The Ta Chung Book Company, 1964. A short autobiography of Li Ch'ing-chao included in the preceding book.

SECONDARY SOURCES

Connaissance de l'Orient. Anthologie de la Póesie Chinoise Classique. Paris: NRF, 1963. A very complete anthology of Chinese poetry with accurate but literal translations.

Encyclópedie de la Pléiade. Histoire des Littératures. Paris: NRF, 1956. A history of world literatures with a chapter devoted to Chinese literature.

Giles, Herbert A. *History of Chinese Literature.* Taipei: The World Book Company, 1963. An introduction to Chinese literature with emphasis laid upon literary translations of original texts.

Hsüeh Li-jo. *Sung Tz'u T'ung Luen.* Taipei: The K'ai Ming Book Company, 1954. Very remarkable commentaries on Sung Tz'u.

Hu Pin-ching (Guillermaz, Patricia). *La Póesie Chinoise.* Paris: Pierre Seghers, 1959. An anthology of Chinese poetry with accurate and literary translations.

Hu Yün-i. *Chung Kuo Tz'u Shih.* Taipei: The Ch'i Ming Book Company, 1956. A detailed history of *tz'u.*

Liu, James. *The Art of Chinese Poetry.* Taipei: The Chin Wen Book Company, 1963. A remarkable survey of the whole structure of Chinese poetry with accurate and literary translations.

Liu Ta-chieh. *Chung Kuo Wen Hsüeh Fa Chan Shih.* Taipei: The Chung Hua Book Company, 1952. The best and most complete history of Chinese literature.

Miao Yüeh. *Shih Tz'u T'ung Luen.* Taipei: The K'ai Ming Book Company, 1954. Very remarkable essays on several Chinese poets and *tz'u* writers with very original views of the nature of poetry and that of *tz'u.*

She Hsueh-man. *Nü Tz'u Jen Li Ch'ing-chao.* Kaoshiung: The Ta

Chung Book Company, 1964. A very remarkable study of Li Ch'ing-chao with annotations of her *tz'u*.

Wang Yün-wu. *Tz'u P'in*. Taipei: The Commercial Press, 1954. Commentaries of *tz'u* assembled by the writer.

Index

APR. 06, 191 2